Coping With
Sexual Harassment

Coping With Sexual Harassment

by
Beryl Black

THE ROSEN PUBLISHING GROUP, INC.
New York

Published in 1987 by The Rosen Publishing Group, Inc.
29 East 21st Street, New York, NY 10010

First Edition

Library of Congress Cataloging-in-Publication Data

Black, Beryl.
    Coping with sexual harassment.

    (Coping)
    Bibliography: p.
    Includes index.
    Summary: Discusses incidents of sexual harassment
experienced by young people and ways of coping with
this problem.
    1. Sexual harassment of women—United States.
2. Sex discrimination in employment—United States.
[1. Sexual harassment]   I. Title.   II. Series.
[DNLM: 1. Interpersonal Relations—popular works.
2. Sex Behavior—popular works.   3. Women's Rights—

popular works.   HD 6060.3 B627c]
HD6060.3.B55   1987   331.13'3   86-26245
ISBN   0-8239-0732-5

Manufactured in the United States of America

Coping With Sexual Harassment

Contents

I.   *The Situation on My New Job—Diary Entry*   1

II.   *Readers' Responses to Ted & Monica*   14

III.   *Kenny's Story—Letter to Ted & Monica*   27

IV.   *Who Is the Harasser?—Ted & Monica's Column*   34

V.   *Diary Entry by Young & Alone*   45

VI.   *Stacy's Story—Letter to Ted & Monica*   53

VII.   *Who Are Victims of Sexual Harassment?—Ted & Monica's Column*   63

VIII.   *Readers' Responses to Ted & Monica*   73

IX.   *Finding Oneself—Ted & Monica's Column*   89

X.   *Power—Ted & Monica's Column*   100

XI.   *What to Do about Sexual Harassment—Ted & Monica's Column*   109

XII.   *Problems in Coping with Sexual Harassment—Ted & Monica's Column*   122

XIII.   *Diary Entry by Young & Alone*   137

Footnotes   144

Bibliography   145

Index   147

Chapter I

The Situation on My New Job— Diary Entry

Dear Diary:

Why am I so worried about that situation at work? Why do I feel that I don't know how to handle it? Am I afraid to lose my first job by telling what I know? Or is it a matter of what I think I know? Is it that I'm really not sure what my supervisor's attentions are all about?

Sure, I think I know as much as any other person my age. I'm not naive. I live in an age when young people are more sexually aware, more socially conscious and sophisticated than at any other time in history. How could I not know what this is all about?

But then, I argue with myself, why do you keep getting snagged on the thought that maybe you're wrong, maybe you're making a big deal out of nothing? After all, this isn't high school; people talk and act differently in the real world, and maybe you just weren't prepared for how different it would be. What if your supervisor is just trying to be nice to you and really means to flatter you? All it means is that you really are attractive, and isn't that what you'd like to hear? Maybe I'm just being a big baby. I wish I had an older sister or brother to talk to about it. I'm scared to death to tell Mom and Dad. Dear Diary, what should I do?

Things I Would Tell My Older Sister or Brother about This Situation (if I had one or if I had the courage to tell)

1. My boss gave me his/her phone number and asked me to call him/her at home.
2. My boss manages to brush against me or touch me several times every shift.
3. My boss says that if certain things go well I will get a better shift or a better station at work.
4. My boss calls me at home and asks for dates.
5. My boss tries to be alone with me at work, has fondled me and tried to kiss me.
6. When my parents were late coming to get me once, my boss tried to get me to wait in his/her car.
7. When I put my boss off, I wind up working the late shift, get yelled at for nothing, and have my breaks taken away.
8. My boss often gets me alone and tries to make dates with me.
9. My boss gets too close to me when we're working, and it makes me feel uncomfortable.
10. My boss says really vulgar things to me when no one else is around.
11. Other people have been fired for no reason when the boss didn't get anywhere with them.

It boils down to this: I want to keep my job; I want to have a good work record; I want to be able to use this, my first job, on my résumé and get a good recommendation from this job. And, I'll have to admit it, I don't know how to handle this situation. What can I do?

I suppose, Diary, that you'd advise me to tell someone, but do you have any idea what that could do? Just think about it. Here are some of the possibilities.

Things My Parents Might Say or Do If I Told Them

1. "You have to quit that job now!" Jobs are really

hard to find, especially for teenagers. Everybody I know was trying to get this job, and I should risk losing it just like that? I'd have to be crazy!

2. They might do something crazy, like a big confrontation with my boss. I'd be embarrassed to death if they did that. And all the other people at work might even hear. "We're going over there now and talk to him/her and you won't ever have any trouble again."

3. They might call the company headquarters and make trouble for my boss. What would I ever do if my boss said I was lying? It's just his/her word against mine. "We'd like to believe you, darling, but this boss of yours seems like such a *nice* person."

4. My parents and friends might not trust me anymore if my boss managed to convince everyone I was lying. "Well, remember the last time you cried wolf and there was nothing to it?"

5. My parents might even think I provoked this situation. They're always saying I try to act too sophisticated!

6. They would definitely have a "serious" talk with me about the dangers out in the world, and I would feel like a baby. "That is the world out there, honey, and you know how we've always sheltered you."

In the meantime, the situation is getting worse and worse. I dread having to go to work; I dread the thought of having to be alone with my boss. I cringe every time he/she smiles that weird smile at me, as if we were partners in some great conspiracy. I actually shiver when he/she walks past me, pauses behind me, or stands next to me. I never know what is coming next, and my fear of my own reaction is part of the whole terrible thing.

You see, part of me seems to like all the attention!

I don't know how to handle that. I know I should be scared or mad or outraged or something. And I do feel some of that outrage, a lot of it actually, but I know that a part of me is interested in seeing just how far this can go without getting serious. There is a little person in me who seems to like this new kind of approval from an older person. It's kind of fascinating to watch myself in something like a TV drama.

But then I realize what I'm thinking, Dear Diary, and I'm ashamed of myself. I wasn't brought up that way. Oh, I am so very confused!

Some Aspects of My Emotional Confusion

I want to be mature enough to handle my own problems. I think I ought to be able to deal with a problem at work.

I wish I could just go to my parents for the answer.

I can't tell my parents! They think I'm still their little child. They would not appreciate this at all.

I want to be an adult, but I don't know if I'm ready yet.

I am frightened by my boss's advances. I don't know if he/she is just kidding and is basically a decent person, or if this is "the *big bad wolf.*"

I wish things were as simple and clear-cut as they were when I was a child. I knew then not to take candy from strangers; this is my boss who is being too sweet.

I get a creepy feeling when my boss talks to me or tries to touch me.

It is kind of flattering to get this adult kind of interest. No one else at

Maybe no one else is noticed in that way because they have too much self-respect or have told the boss to "get lost."

It could be that everyone is secretly laughing at me, waiting to see what a jerk I'll make of myself.

I feel like I'm a dirty joke.

Yuk!

What if I came to really love my boss?

What would I do when it was all over? Commit suicide? Get another job and another lover? Get married?

What if I get someone to listen to me and everyone at work says I encouraged the boss? What if it's my fault?

work seems to be noticed by the boss like that.

Maybe the boss has gone after me because it is obvious how insecure and scared I am, and I seem to be an "easy mark."

On the other hand, maybe I'm the first person this boss has been so attracted to. It *is* kind of exciting.

Maybe a real affair with an older person is the best way to start off my sex life. After all, what harm can it do me, and I might learn a lot.

What if I am being used?

What if my boss dumped me, is married, or has another lover?

Am I going to let it start? The whole thing makes me feel ill, and I do not want it to happen. *Help me!*

What can I do? I feel so lonely!

I try to imagine what I would do if this were a TV sitcom and I were the principal writer. How would I write the young hero/heroine out of this mess? How would it be handled on my favorite show? What would Bill Cosby and his kids do about it? Could Michael J. Fox deal with sexual harassment on the job?

If I could let my fantasy go to work for me, Diary, I'd think of some great ways to let my boss see how things are. There are definite possibilities along that line.

1. I could go wired to work. That, however, would not catch all the handwork my boss does, all the little pats on the butt.
2. I could hire some friends to do a "hit" on the boss: dump manure on his/her car; send a singing telegram, with the message of what kind of person he/she is spelled out good; make an "accident" happen to him/her.
3. I could speak up to the boss myself. That is probably how the Cosby kids or Michael J. would handle it in the first place.
4. If that didn't work, I could draw up the big guns, Mom and Dad, the company management, the courts, the newspapers. (What a fantasy!)

I know I must speak up to him/her myself, much as I'd rather like to see a load of manure dumped on the boss's car (or on the boss). I might feel guilty for the rest of my life if I caused a real accident to happen to him/her. How do I get the guts to talk to my boss, to get my boss to take me seriously?

Scenario 1

ME: Good morning, Boss, I'd like to talk to you about

a matter I consider very important. In fact, this matter has been giving me cause for some negative preoccupation and undue mental stress for quite some time now. I'm afraid matters have gotten to the point where I feel the need to address this issue with you directly and therefore . . .

BOSS: (going out door) Sorry, kid, you've taken up too much of my time. (Returning to put arm around me) How about us getting together after work? We could go someplace quiet, just you and me, and you can tell me all about your stress . . . (goes out, closing door).

ME: NO, no, no!

Scenario 2

ME: Boss, from now on keep your hands off me and leave me alone or I'll report you to your superiors.

BOSS: I'll leave you alone all right! You're fired!

Scenario 3

ME: I need this job, but I'm not going to let you take advantage of me the way you have been.

BOSS: I'm sorry I got out of line. You're absolutely right, and I apologize.

Scenario 4

ME: Look, you creep, don't ever get out of line with me again. If you ever make smart remarks to me again or touch my body, I swear I'll see that you get taken care of. I have friends who care a lot about me, and they won't like what's been happening here. And, believe me, they can get wild when they have a mind to.

BOSS: Please! Gosh! I didn't mean anything—really! You've got me all wrong; I'm not that kind of person at all. I'm just a great kidder, that's all. I promise you there won't be anything ever again to make you think I've gotten the least little bit out of line. And, oh, by the way, starting next week there will be a $.75 per hour increase in your paycheck. I've been meaning to tell you for some time but just haven't gotten around to it. Not that it has anything to do with what you were talking about or anything. Nothing at all! Thanks for coming to me about your concern. I'm sure I'll improve; I really will!

Scenario 5

ME: Boss, I've got your supervisor and my lawyer here with me. I'm suing you for sexual harassment on the job to the tune of $200,000.

BOSS: (faints)

Those are interesting scenarios, especially the last three. However, what if, Scenario 5 turned out like this:

Scenario 6

ME: Boss, I've got your supervisor and my lawyer here because I'm suing you for sexual harassment on the job to the tune of $200,000.

BOSS: Look, kid, go ahead and sue. I've got the goods on you, and I'll countersue. I haven't said or done anything to you that you haven't asked for, and I've got proof. When I'm done with you, you and your folks won't have a penny left and you won't be able to hold your head up in public.

Well, it's obvious that I need help. I need to bounce my fears and frustrations off someone. I can write to you, Diary, and that helps some. Just putting it all down on paper helps quite a bit actually, but I wish you could give me some feedback. I need an advice specialist, and I need, for obvious reasons, to remain anonymous. What better way, Dear Diary, for me to do both those things than to write to the "TED & MONICA" column in the paper? Who knows? Maybe I'll get a good answer from them or from their readers.

Dear Ted & Monica:

I have a problem I'm really ashamed to talk about. I am a teenager; I won't tell you whether I'm a girl or a boy to help protect my identity (actually this sort of thing can happen to anybody).

I just started my first job, and already I'm having trouble. My boss (again I won't say if it is a male or female. I'm sure this kind of thing isn't limited to either sex). That's what I have to talk to you about—sex—my boss has started coming on to me, and I'm afraid.

I'm afraid for all sorts of reasons. I don't want to lose my job. I want to have a good-looking résumé some day with lots of excellent recommendations; I don't want to make a bust of my first job. I want my boss to like me, but not in that way. Part of me, however, is actually a little flattered at the attention I'm getting.

I'm scared to tell my parents. I'm terrified of what their reaction might be. You know, maybe this is just nothing, and I wouldn't want them to overreact. Maybe I'm misreading the whole thing and this is how people behave in the job world. I mean, I'm still in high school and have very little experience with this sort of thing, none really.

I suppose I should talk to my boss, but I don't know

how. I'm scared to death. What really scares me, however, is how far it might go and what it might lead to if I don't say or do something. Maybe I seem more sophisticated than I really am. There is a lot of difference, I see, between looking grown-up and being mature enough to handle situations.

I feel like I'm being a baby. Maybe I should just ignore the whole thing and it will go away. Sometimes I think the entire episode is just a figment of my imagination.

However, it is a reality that my boss has asked me to go out with him/her. It is also a reality that I feel very uncomfortable around my boss. He/she always makes remarks that embarrass me. I wouldn't let my friends at school talk to me like that.

No one has ever brushed against me the way my boss does either. There are times when I am sure the boss is trying to get a good feel. There are other times when the boss has patted me on the behind in a way that I don't like. I think the boss has the idea that I like all this. I'm afraid of where it may lead.

I have no one to talk to, no older brothers and sisters. I could go to the school counselor, but I'm too embarrassed. Besides, what can school counselors do? They're always so busy with scheduling and whatnot that I don't feel comfortable going in with something like this. I *have* been writing in my diary and that helps, but my diary can't talk back.

It was because of writing in my diary that I thought of consulting you, though, so maybe I get more feedback from my diary than I realized. Maybe I communicate with myself through my diary. That's a great thought, and I suddenly don't feel so lonely anymore.

Please give me some advice. I really am desperate for help. You see, the boss has never actually come right out and said, "If you do this, I will do these things for you here at work." Nor has he/she ever said, "If you don't give me what I want, don't expect any advancement around here; don't even expect to keep your job!" I just have a gut feeling that that is what it is all about.

I especially feel that way because my work is not as good as it was before all this started. I seem to mess up a lot more now. I get so nervous when my boss is around that I fumble and bumble. And then, to make it all worse, my boss is so reassuring, overly nice. The other night he/she asked me if I wanted to stay after everyone left and go over the procedure more thoroughly. I was so terrified that I blurted out: "Which procedure?" I'm sure I looked like a fool and sounded like one, too. My boss just smiled, got so close to me I could scarcely move without touching him/her, and said, "Oh, you know, this procedure." Then he/she touched my arm and pointed to my work. I backed away and said I couldn't stay; I had to be home.

I suppose people get used to this. I'm sure (from what I've read and seen on TV) that lots of people get ahead this way. I just don't know if I'm ready to start a lifetime of sleeping around to keep my job or to get ahead in my career.

There is no one at work I can trust enough to ask if this kind of thing goes on regularly with new people. Am I just the "new kid on the job," the one who has to be "broken in" (literally)?

I sort of get the feeling that everyone else at work is a little distrustful of me, a little resentful. Maybe that is because of my boss's attentions. Maybe, on the other hand, I'm just paranoid. Please help me. I need to hear from someone. Sign me,

Young & Alone on a New Job

Dear Young & Alone on a New Job:

Your letter is so full of things we thought might be of interest and helpful to many young people starting jobs that we decided to print it in its entirety, which we rarely do. The first thing we want to tell you is that you are not alone. Not only are there other people who share your fears and frustrations on the job, but there are others who are the victims of subtle harassment in much the same way you are being victimized.

The simplest thing might be for you to get another job. However, as you suggest, that is not always easy, given the job market and the unemployment rate of present times. It would be better for you to learn to deal with a problem like this right from the start of your career as an employee, as there may be many times when you will need those skills. You may never face the same problem again, but if you possess the skills to handle this one you can deal with many other problems a little more easily.

As you note, many people do use sexual favors to gain career goal objectives. That is nothing new, and it should not be surprising to you. It is a common practice both in the white-collar business world and in the world of blue-collar workers. This may come as a surprise to you, but it happens in high schools, too. There are teachers, coaches, and administrative personnel (of both sexes, as you point out) who manipulate young persons for their own sexual gain.

We would like to help you more significantly than we can do in just one answer to your request for help. Therefore, we have decided to devote a portion of the space in this column over the next few weeks to this problem of how to cope with sexual harassment. Continue to dialogue with us during this time, if you wish to do so. Your desire for anonymity is certainly secure, and the dialogue may be beneficial both to you and to us in that the continuing feedback will occasion greater creativity in dealing with the issue. We also invite our readers to respond to you. We feel that our readers' insights are often extremely beneficial to our correspondents.

So, you readers out there, how would you answer Young & Alone on a New Job? What advice would you give this young person starting out in the world of work? If you have had similar experiences that you care to share, we will respect your right to remain anonymous. If you have stories to tell that are too long for the column, we will print what we can and send your entire letter to Young & Alone. Or we can send your letter on to Young & Alone without printing any of it, if that is your request.

What do you say, readers? We've always relied on you for marvelous common-sense responses to our questioners. Don't let us down now. What would you like to tell this young person about a problem that must be as old as the world?

Ted & Monica

Chapter II

Readers' Responses to Ted & Monica

Dear Ted & Monica:

Please send my letter to Young & Alone on a New Job. I know just how she (or he) feels. I once quit a job because I was always getting pawed by my boss. He thought it was funny, I guess. No matter where I was or what I was doing he'd come up behind me and poke me—in the ribs, in the arm, on the fanny—anywhere.

I didn't appreciate it, and I told him so. I finally quit, and I told him I didn't come to work to be pawed all over. I told him I didn't enjoy it one bit. He just looked at me as if I was crazy.

Take my advice, Young & Alone. Don't let anyone—not anyone at all—do things to you that you think are wrong. Just don't take it and stand up for yourself!

Patty "No-Paws"

Dear Young & Alone:

If I were you I'd pull back my senses. I mean I'd really stand back and get a grip on myself. Then I might murder the guy or whoever it was trying to put the make on me. It would really shock me. But when I'd got my senses back in order again, I'd take action. Believe me, I would.

I might really try to murder someone for doing something like that to me. At least I'd get another job. Who cares about a recommendation from a creep like that?

I say you should pull back your senses and take a real good look at this whole situation. I don't think you realize how serious it is. Do you want everybody your whole life to make a fool out of you? What are you trying to be, the guy's mother? You can't be a mother to someone who's walking all over you. You can't even be nice to someone who's walking all over you. And you sure can't do a good job when you're always looking over your shoulder to see when you're going to be attacked.

Action-Taker

Dear Young & Alone on a New Job:

It happens all the time. People just don't talk about it. Nobody talks about it. This kind of thing might not lead to actual sex or even sexual abuse, but the harassment goes on all the time. If my mother and father had known what I had to go through when I first started my job, they would have come and got me right there on the spot.

But you very rarely get people to talk about this, to admit that it happens. Why is that, do you suppose? Most young kids are like you, Y & A. They're scared. They think it's their fault. Now I ask you, is it your fault that you're young, that you might possibly be good-looking also? Is it your fault that you happen to be in the wrong place at the wrong time? I wonder, Y & A, just how many others at your work have been harassed by this "person" (so-called) before you? Did you really think you might be the "one and only"?

Now think of all the possible reasons why they might not tell you if they have been harassed or if they see what is happening to you. One is—maybe they're jealous. Yes, that's what I said—maybe they're jealous.

You never know what makes some people tick, Y & A. One person's turn-on may give another person chills, so to speak. (And vice versa, I might add.) Or, who knows, maybe they've been rejected by this "person" so-called. Maybe they've already had their little fling with the boss and you're the "new kid at the hungry-heartbreak banquet table."

Maybe, just maybe, everyone else thinks you're pretty cool. Maybe you look like you're handling yourself pretty well and don't need any help. Some people give that impression, you know, even when they're falling apart inside. You might look like you wouldn't welcome anyone else's interference or advice. On the other hand, you may have everyone guessing. They might think you like the boss's attentions. If that were the case they would stay out of it, because you might tell the boss on them if they stuck their noses into your business.

Then there are always people who are scared to do something about evil. You know them. They're the ones who are afraid to speak up, afraid to interfere in other people's business even when they know something is going on that's wrong. I guess they feel everyone has a right to some private evil as long as it doesn't involve them directly.

Well, Young & Alone, may the wind (as they say in Ireland) be always at your back—but may it not be the hot breath of your lecherous boss breathing down your neck.

Had Experience

Dear Young & Alone:

I was so glad to see your letter in the paper. Don't get me wrong. I don't mean that I'm glad you're going through this. That's an awful thing to wish on anyone. What I mean is, I'm glad because I see that this is a big thing to someone else besides me. I'm so tired of all the nasty little remarks I've had to take from my boss over the last year that it's almost a relief to realize I'm not alone. I'm almost grateful to have company in my misery. I hope you don't misunderstand me. I do know what you are going through. It's just that I haven't had anyone to talk to about this, and your letter was like the hand of a friend reaching out to give me strength.

Sometimes I feel about people like your boss and mine as if they were like children in big bodies. I resent that we have to work for people who are underdeveloped as human beings. I have stayed at this job, but I also have developed an ulcer, am taking medicine daily for it, and am a nervous wreck. I wish I had had the good sense to ask for advice as you are doing, but, even then, I don't know whether or not I would have taken it. I felt I needed the money so badly that I just had to stay on this job. I've got kids to feed, and I'm the only one there is to bring in money. Sign me,

Chicken

Dear Ted & Monica:

Please encourage Young & Alone to get help from a counselor or to go to his/her parents. You can't go through these things without some kind of advice. It's sort of like watching a game show (only I realize this is a serious thing). However, during a game show you can sit in your living room and watch what's happening and the answer can come to you just like that. You know what I'm talking about. It's happened to all of us, I think.

But when you're right there in that studio, it's a different thing altogether. I know, because I participated in one once. I was on "$1,000,000 Chance of a Lifetime." You are so close to the clues that you can't get a good perspective of the whole word. At home I could always get those words without any trouble. I guess it was because there was enough distance between me and the game for my perspective to get right.

That's why I think Young & Alone needs to get some distance, some perspective, if he or she is to solve this problem. Going to a counselor can help to give you that perspective. Maybe the school counselors don't do that sort of thing anymore, but there are all kinds of clinics and referral services. I'm sure Young & Alone could find some of them in the phone book or from some crisis hot line. There must be some place where young people can go to get these answers.

I think young people nowadays must have many more problems to face than we did when we were youngsters. I think we need to provide all the help we can for them. It is dreadful to think our youngsters have to face things that are hard even for older people to handle.

From Another Generation

Dear Young & Alone:

You young people make me sick. You want it all your own way. You want to have your cake and eat it too. You want to have your fun, get your cheap little thrills, but stay good and pure. I've had people like you working for me.

A person tries to make the workplace pleasant, kid around a little bit, and you all go running off and yelling "Rape." You make me sick, you really do. If I had it my way, I'd never hire another teenager, but then I'd be hauled into court on some kind of "discrimination" charges or something. You can't win for losing.

I see you come into my store year after year. You all get slicker and smarter and snottier year after year. If you were my kids I'd do something about the way you dress, the way you talk, and the way you carry yourselves. You act as if you've been out on the streets soliciting for years, and then when someone brushes against your elbow in passing, you go into hysterics. You act like you've been having sex since you were six years old and there isn't anything you don't know about the subject. The way you dress is guaranteed to make the looker think about just one thing. However, when someone stares at the wrapping you've plastered around your "goodies," you get offended. Talk about double standards! You kids send double messages, let me tell you!

One message says: "Oh, take me! Take me! I'm yours for the taking! Anyone! Take me!"

The other message comes across: "I'm just a poor little innocent. Please excuse the way I talk, dress, and walk. This is just how I want to act grown-up. I'm really shy and childlike!"

My advice to you, Young & Alone, is to take a good look at yourself. If you're sending out these double messages, you have only yourself to blame for your predicament. It takes two to tango, as they say, kid.

Sick of Teenage Vamps

Dear Ted & Monica:

I can't believe anyone is really as naive as this Young & Alone pretends to be. Are you sure that letter wasn't a little joke of the "Yale boys"?

You can't tell me that there are any young people in the world today who don't know how to handle every possible situation that comes along. You see, Ted & Monica, I'm the mother of three teenagers, two girls and a boy, and I've been convinced for years that parents are obsolete.

My kids know everything and can handle everything (or so they would have me believe). They rely on me only for such things as hot food, clean clothes, and chauffeuring to all their various appointments. Other than that, they can take care of themselves, thank you. I would give anything for a real heart-to-heart with one of them.

The other night I thought I could use Young & Alone's letter as a jumping-off point for a discussion, but I was mistaken. When I introduced the subject, they laughed and laughed. They made a big joke of the whole thing and then started lecturing *me* about sexual harassment on my job—their home! Then they turned to their father and called him a dirty old man for smooching me while I was frying the chicken.

I doubt that Young & Alone was any more serious than my own teenagers. I think, Ted & Monica, that you've been had. I think today's teenagers can handle just about anything they put their minds to.

Successful Mother of Satisfied Teens

Dear Ted & Monica:

How my heart goes out to Young & Alone. I am the mother of two young men just recently out of their teens. Both of them have experienced what Young & Alone is talking about, although each in very different circumstances.

My one son is in the Navy, and he was approached by an officer, another man, while on duty aboard ship. What could he do? He was so young and thousands of miles from home. Somehow the same rules, the same guidelines and guarantees of protection don't seem to operate away from the home "nest." I could almost cry now when I am reminded of how hard it has been for him.

My son had been a "model" in the Navy. He had been honored several times for his conduct and attentiveness to duty. All he wanted in life was to be a career Navy officer. That's all he had ever talked about as a little boy. He had never, even in high school, done things like other boys, smoke dope or things like that.

Well, he refused this man's overt attentions; he rejected this older officer altogether. He must have had some idea of what would be the consequences of doing that. Within a week of his telling this officer in no uncertain terms that he wanted nothing to do with him sexually, someone "found" a large cache of hard drugs in my son's mattress. Well, to make a long story short, he was court-martialed and is in a federal penitentiary serving a twelve-year sentence. His life is ruined.

My other son went to work as a paralegal while still in law school. Well, a woman attorney in the firm where he worked had her eyes on him. She was after him constantly to go to bed with her. When he did have an affair with her, it consumed him entirely. His work suffered, his grades dropped, and he flunked the bar exam. He lost his job, of course. Now he is trying to rebuild his life. I am very bitter when I think of what has happened to both my sons.

Of course, I realize that each person is responsible for his/her own conduct, but I see, too, that temptations are put in the way of the young that they are totally incapable of handling without help and guidance. My sons needed help from someone on the outside, someone who could be objective with them. I was so protective of them that they could predetermine what I would have told them.

I hope Young & Alone gets help before it is too late.
                                    A Mother Who Understands

Dear Young & Alone on a New Job:
Why should you be any different from the rest of us?

Year after year, "innocent" young teens go into the marketplace looking for opportunities to make money, to become wealthy, to dress well and buy nice cars.

Well, welcome to the world of work, honey. This is the way it is now, ever has been, and ever shall be. Amen!

Miss Ann Thropic

Dear Young & Alone:

I am a personnel director of a large fast-food chain, and I can assure you that we do not tolerate the kind of behavior you describe from any of our managers. We have a regular process by which you may file a complaint. Everything is kept confidential, and the matter is carefully investigated.

We have had very few complaints such as yours in the five years that I have held this position, but the few instances that I recall were solved satisfactorily.

In one instance there was no proof that the manager had, in fact, been guilty of any misconduct. In the other case, the manager was dismissed, and an equitable damage remuneration was made to the victim out of court.

I strongly urge you to take steps through the proper channels to insure speedy resolution of your problem.

Sincerely yours,
Candace Chanamara

Dear Young & Alone:

I know your type. You're out to make a killing on this, aren't you? What is it, the money or the kicks that you're after? You young people are all alike. You've been spoiled all your lives and you come along and try to wreck someone else's life with your filthy little tricks. Are you talking about reality or something you'd like to have happen, sweetheart?

Maybe you've had this dream, see, and you have a
fantasy life built up involving your boss. Well, step out
of your fantasy and see the reality before you destroy
someone's life like mine was destroyed by one of you
spoiled kids.

Some little liar messed me up for good with a story of
how I had "sexually harassed" her!

Been There

Dear Young & Alone:

You sound like you're too young to have a job yet. Fly
back into your nest until you grow up.

No Fledgling

Dear Young & Alone:

Some people just happen to like young people. So
what's wrong with that?

True Blue

Dear Ted & Monica:

Who is Young & Alone kidding anyway? Everybody
knows that young people aren't virgins anymore probably after they get out of eighth grade. I mean, what's all
this talk about "babies having babies" if teenagers are so
prudish, so proper, and so protected?

Come off it, Ted & Monica. I gave you credit for
more sense than to be suckered into something like this.
Today's teens are having sex, having babies or having
abortions. You can't tell me that a little pinch on the ·
butt or a little feel is going to scare them as witless as
this Young & Alone is trying to appear.

Skeptical Scarlett

Dear Young & Alone:

I can't imagine that you don't know how to handle this

yourself. I am a teenager, and you'd better believe no one is going to touch my body without my permission! A guy at school came up to me while I was at my locker and tried to get a feel on me. I turned around and grabbed him and pushed him up against the lockers.

I told him if he ever did anything like that to me again I'd fix him so he couldn't walk for a week. Then I went to the principal and said, "Listen, I've been in this school for almost four years, I've never had a discipline referral and never caused one bit of trouble. Now I'm coming to you and I'm telling you that something had better be done about this guy because I won't let people go around touching my body like that. It's my body, and I say who can touch me or not." Then I went to my counselor and said pretty much the same thing. Later that day the kid came up to apologize to me. That was as he was on his way out the door for a three-day suspension for what he'd done to me.

There are other kids I know who wouldn't have made such a fuss, but I think they're crazy. If you don't stand up for yourself, no one else is going to do a single thing for you. I got action because I made it very clear that I was not going to be treated like that.

I realize this was another kid, and Young & Alone is talking about something that happened on the job. I think I would have done just about the same thing if I had been on the job and been harassed like that.

No Hands on Hannah

Dear Young & Alone:

I think I know just how you feel. Once I went to a movie by myself and this guy sitting next to me put his hand on my leg. I was so shocked I didn't know what to do. I didn't want to make a fuss. I didn't want to yell or go get the usher or the manager. I felt like a fool. All I did was shrink away from his touch and move into the farthest corner of my seat like a frightened animal. I didn't even have the nerve to get up and change seats, I was that embarrassed.

Later, when I told my friends, they yelled at me for not having taken more direct action. I had simply been too hurt and humiliated to do anything. I just couldn't believe anything so awful was really happening to me. You only read about stuff like that happening to other people. I remember feeling so dumb, so dirty. I wanted to cry. I felt like the man was making a horrible mistake. I had always been a good person, and I wasn't anything like what he must be thinking. Just because I was alone didn't mean I was desperate.

Good Girl

Dear Ted & Monica:
So what's wrong with a little fun and games on the job? It adds a little spice to your work, and no one gets hurt by it. We've always done a little teasing where I work, and everyone who's there gets so they can give and take.

Ready to Party

Dear Ted & Monica:
It may be that this is just a once-in-a-lifetime kind of thing, but my best friend at work was murdered by her floor manager when she refused to go out with him. He's awaiting execution now.

He and three of his friends abducted her when she went on her lunch break. It was his day off, and it was the day when she always went to the bank instead of having lunch with her friends. They followed her and abducted her in the bank parking lot. They took her by boat to a nearby island, raped her, and killed her.

She couldn't stand him, and he hated her for it. He gave her the creeps. She always told him to get lost and leave her alone, that she had a fiancé. We used to laugh about him when we were all together for lunch. Maybe that's what we did wrong. We never took him seriously.

I'd give anything to have her back now. I was to be the maid of honor at her wedding in the fall. I can't get the memories out of my head, and I try to figure how it could have gone differently. I know I should just realize that this guy (and his friends) were crazy. They were drunk and probably high on drugs and just out to get revenge. But how many crazies are there out there? That's what scares me. You never really know who you're dealing with. Even crazies can act fairly normal a good part of the time.

Bereft

Dear Ted & Monica:

Young & Alone sure has a problem. I mean if he or she can't just tell someone to bug off, that's really a problem, isn't it?

Any girl I go out with sure let's me know if she wants me to do it to her. I have my regular woman and I do it to her—whenever. But I think if some chick told me not to do it to her, I'd get the message.

Young & Alone hasn't been around very long, it looks like to me. There are ways of dealing with everything.

Mister Cool

Chapter III

Kenny's Story—Letter to Ted & Monica

Dear Young & Alone:

We are very grateful to have your address and hope that some of the material we are sending you from our readers may prove helpful to you. Most of what we receive we can simply put in our column for all our readers to see, but several items have come in regarding your situation that we preferred to pass directly to you without printing them.

We were very intrigued by this story, the story of Kenny, which he sent us from prison.

Affectionately,
Ted & Monica

Kenny's Story

Dear Ted & Monica:

I read your column in the newspaper every day. I am in the State Penitentiary here, and I always look in your column. It helps me to know other people have problems too. I was so interested in that letter you had from the kid on the first job. The one about the sexual harassment.

That was like looking at myself in a mirror. It was my story, only I hope that kid don't wind up like I did.

I'll be up for parole in a few more years. I'll probably get it too, as I've done pretty good in here so far. No trouble, that is. I'd like to say some things to Young & Alone, but I wouldn't want you to print it in the paper. I wouldn't want to hurt my folks any more than I've already hurt them, so maybe if you could send this on to Young & Alone, I can do somebody some good somehow.

I was a junior in high school when I went looking for work. Only I didn't look for no ordinary kind of jobs like most kids did, the McDonald's jobs and all that. I couldn't handle working in no restaurant, the hours they work, and all you have to take off of everybody, the managers, the other workers, and the customers even.

So I went to work for this guy. He lived in my neighborhood and had his own business laying carpet and linoleum. He was pretty well thought of by everyone, as he was a Vietnam hero and all that. And he told me we could make big money. It looked good to me.

I even cut school some to go to work with him when there were jobs. And I can tell you I was making good money. I had never had it so good. I could give money to my younger sister for clothes for school. I even bought her prom dress.

Well, he pretty much split the money fifty-fifty with me, which I thought was fantastic. He didn't have to do that. I was just a kid. Well, he must have been thinking the same thing, because before long he come to me wanting more for his money, if you know what I mean. Now I wasn't that kind of guy. It's pretty hard on you at school if the kids think you're gay or anything. Besides, I knew I wasn't. I'd had girlfriends and never thought about doing things with any guy. But he told me like it was. If I wanted to keep all that good money rolling in, I'd better do some rolling of my own—with him in the sack. I put it off and put it off. Finally he told me he had a new kid coming in to take my job, that he'd still rather have me, in bed as well as on the job, but I'd best make up my mind.

Well, of course, that got to me. I'll never know for sure if there really was another guy coming in. I never could get him to tell me the kid's name. I've always had my doubts that there ever was anyone else. He just tried to get to me, tried to scare me. That was what done him in finally. But I'll get to that.

So I started making love with this guy. At first I kept my girlfriend and tried to act like everything was the same as always. But it wasn't. My whole life was changed. I even began to get jealous of this guy. And he knew how to make me jealous. If I went to school he'd let me think someone had been there while I was gone. So I started staying home more and more. And the more I stayed home from school, the less work we did. Pretty soon we weren't hardly laying any more carpets and stuff, we were so busy getting laid ourselves. That meant no more money was coming in, and the only reason I had done this in the first place was because of the money and the job.

But I couldn't get away from him. Whenever he'd see that I was ready to complain, we'd do a job and I'd get my regular cut. That would keep me happy for a while. And quiet. I'd go on with him like nothing had happened until the money ran out. I knew I should get out of this, but I didn't know how. Besides I was kind of different now, and everybody was beginning to notice it.

Well, for one thing, I failed my junior year, and that just about killed me. I didn't want to go back at all, but my mom begged me to. My dad really wanted me to go to college. And I could have. My writing isn't so good now, but you have to remember my schooling was cut short. So I started my junior year over again in the fall. That's about all I did was start it, because all the same old stuff began again, and I knew that to keep this guy I had to cut school. Yes, by this time I had admitted to myself that it was him I wanted now, and not just the job or the money. Because, let's face it, I could have gotten another job if that's all it was. But I was hooked, and I guess that's what he had counted on. But once he realized he had me, he acted different, and that's when things changed for me.

He really started getting other guys in then. Unless I was there with him every minute, I couldn't be sure that he wouldn't have someone else. And there were other kids working for him now. I hardly got any money. Suddenly I knew I had to get out of this. I told him so. I told him I needed to get regular work and that I was going to look for a job. A friend of mine told me there was an opening at McDonald's, and I was going there for an interview.

When I told this guy I was going for the interview and that I wouldn't be back, he just laughed at me. Then when I started putting my things that I had there in a plastic bag to take home, he said if I ever left him he'd go straight to my parents and tell them the whole thing. He started to call them. He had the phone in his hand. I lost my head or I found it all at once, I don't know which. But I did know one thing for sure. My parents were not going to be brought into this. I loved my family, and they were not going to know what I had done and what I had turned into. It would kill them, I knew. And my sister in school. How could she face that? You know, Young & Alone, what high school kids are like. I don't have to tell you. They'd really get off on this homosexual stuff, and my sister wouldn't be able to survive. She'd be buried alive in the meanness about it. Of course, what they had to live with in the end was a thousand times worse. They not only found out everything I didn't want them to, but there was the murder to hang around their necks too.

So I did the only thing I could. I could hear him dialing. To this day I don't know who he was calling. It could have been the time and temperature number for all I know. Anyway, he had me convinced he was calling my home. I found out afterwards that my mom and dad weren't even home when he was supposedly phoning them. They had taken my sister to the movies; then they all went to a restaurant to eat. That was their last treat for a long time. The police were waiting for them when they got home.

Because I shot him. I shot him right while he had the phone in his hand. Then I hung up the phone. I was afraid that if he had actually reached my number they'd connect the shooting to me. The murder. I watched him die. I felt sorry then, sorry for the whole rotten mess. Sorry for everything I'd done that had led up to a man's getting killed. But I couldn't stand around feeling sorry. I had to fix things so it wouldn't look as if I'd done it. I had to make it look like a robbery. I had to have a chance to get away and be the good person, the member of my family that had always been a good boy. But I didn't get a chance. Even as I raced around trying to throw things here and there, make it look like a robbery, I ran right into a policeman standing in a doorway. I hadn't even heard him come in, I'd been so crazy. The neighbors had called the cops, and it was all over.

And it all came out, and I had hurt my family so terribly. I know it has just about killed my mom and dad, the whole thing, everything I was doing before that led up to the murder, and the murder itself. My sister cried and cried for days and wouldn't go out. They've been good, though. They come to see me and they still love me. If only I had gone to them. If only the job, the money hadn't meant so much to me. When I read this bit in the paper about you, Young & Alone, I couldn't help thinking about how it all got started with me. I just felt like talking about it to someone. I know this is all pretty horrible and far worse than your situation could probably get. But you never know.

I don't know which I feel worse about, what I did to him, killing him like that, or what I did with him before I killed him. I know that he had control of me, and I didn't like it. I know that I felt used and finally just used up. I didn't feel human anymore. I didn't feel like I had control of my own life. Taking that gun in my hands was the first act of getting control back that I had done in a long time. Things had gone so far that nothing short of shooting him would give me back my life, it seemed. I don't know if I actually meant to kill him. Probably.

Anyway, good luck to you, Young & Alone. I'm glad you had sense enough to write to Ted & Monica. I wish I'd done something like that—or gone to someone for help. But I was too ashamed. I couldn't talk about it to anyone. I kept it all inside, and believe me, that's not good. The best thing is to talk it out with someone you can trust. And I had people I could have trusted too. My folks, for one. I was just too embarrassed.

And don't let anyone give you any stuff about being sick or dumb or naive or anything like that. I've read some of those answers people have written in to you, and I can tell you right now some of them don't know what they're talking about. That guy, for instance, who yelled at you for being young and wanting it both ways. He doesn't know what he's talking about. Don't even listen to junk like that. That's just the nutty stuff that comes from a mean old man who's probably so down on life himself that he can't see anything good in anybody. If you've got good parents like I do, talk to them. Better to give them a little grief now than a nightmare later on.

Finally, thanks Ted & Monica, for giving me the chance to get some of this stuff off my chest. It was hard to write it all down, but I feel like the sun has come out in my soul after it's been raining inside me for years. It did me good. I know there are lots of errors in grammar and all in this letter, but that's the least of my worries now, isn't it? You don't know how much your column means to me. It seems like all of us on this earth are more alike than different, don't it? I mean, we're all built pretty much the same way and we have pretty much the same troubles. That's what I wanted to get across to Young & Alone. Sexual harassment is bad enough, but it can lead to some awful consequences—for everybody concerned. The worst thing to do is to keep quiet about it out of fear or ignorance.

Kenny

Chapter IV

Who Is the Harasser?
Ted & Monica's Column

Dear Readers:

We promised you a few columns devoted to the matter of sexual harassment. Since we received the letter from Young & Alone on a New Job, we have been deluged with correspondence from our readers. Some people have requested that their letters, which they consider contain far too intimate revelations for publication, should go directly to Young & Alone. We have cooperated with those requests, printing only the letters that were directed to all our readers.

We have also done considerable research of our own, relying on the wonderful resources in the counseling and legal community for much of our information. We have gone to our friends who are lawyers, psychologists, psychiatrists, and therapeutic social workers for guidance to bring you, our readers, some facts about the people involved in sexual harassment and the nature of harassment itself.

As we have done in the past, we will emulate other nationally known advice columnists in our method of presenting the facts. Although we agree on the main points of the issue, we have some significantly differing views in certain areas of sexual harassment. Thus, we shall present our views in separate sections of the column. We shall, as it were, carry on a discussion for your benefit. In that way we hope to shed as much light as possible on a subject about which, we find, there is very little concrete information. Today's column is devoted to the topic of the person who does the harassing. What kind of person is he/she? Are there certain traits that we can pinpoint in the aggressor?

Monica's Views of the Sexual Harasser

I believe sexual harassment is about *power*. Those who perpetrate this kind of harassment simply want to exert power over their victim. It is not so much an issue of sex as it is a play for power. They want to see how far they can go and how deeply they can abase another individual. They want to frighten and confuse their victim; they want to cause hurt, pain, and confusion.

The desire to hurt may not involve overt sexual acts at all. Just the implicit suggestion, the threat, that actual physical acts could be possible somewhere down the road gets enough results for some aggressors. It is sufficient for them to watch with pleasure the fear that another suffers. They are predatory beasts, and their main enjoyment is the game of stalking their prey, inflicting just enough bite with their bark to terrify their victim.

I am reminded of the classic short story by Charles W. Chesnutt, one of the first great black writers in this country. His story "Dave's Necklace" tells of the tremendous power wielded by the plantation's white overseer, and how he was able to use that power to drive the slave to insanity and suicide. He so dehumanized Dave that Dave became the ham that the overseer had chained around his neck. When Dave hung himself in the smokehouse with the other hams, he only brought to an inevitable conclusion his dehumanization into a "ham."

Sexual harassment is dehumanizing. It has less to do with sexual stimulation or the desire for someone's body than with the desire to have one's will with another, to conquer and subjugate the other. It is like slavery. It stems from the need to control and to maintain control by means of fear. The victim in sexual harassment, like Dave the slave, is humiliated and stripped of the human right to decency. Hatred for the victim is involved in the decision to use this kind of power, and the exercise of the power often leads to violence.

Dave, in Chesnutt's story, was the one slave on the plantation who could read. He read from the Bible that the master had given him. The overseer could not read, and he hated Dave for the superiority that reading gave him. The overseer hated Dave for the Bible that the master had given him. He hated Dave for his goodness and his innocence. He longed for a chance to prove that Dave was corrupt, and he eventually set in motion the machinery to fake evidence that indeed Dave was just as bad as the rest of men. Dave's death was a violent act, and it was the overseer's violence that caused it. The violence had to do with the decision to corrupt Dave.

Sexual harassment is an attempt to corrupt, to offer the apple to an innocent babe. The provider of the apple then becomes the controller, the one looked to for the provision of all other apples. For someone in the workplace those apples might include better hours, a good contract, higher wages, better fringe benefits, better working conditions, promotions. In a school or college setting, the apples could be better grades, a place on the first-string team, a free class period, no exams, no homework, no papers due, a scholarship, higher class rating. The rewarding apples for military persons include promotions, better assignments, better living conditions on or off base. Sexual harassment does not always lead to rape or death, but the will to corrupt is violent at the core.

If Dave had· cringed before his overseer, if he had played the game more cagily, if he had been a match for the cunning and viciousness of the overseer, he might have known how to deal with the white man's hatred for him. Dave chose not to do that; he chose to be the man he knew himself to be. He believed what he had read in the Bible and wanted to be a just man. However, given the system of slavery, Dave could never have realized the full dignity of his humanity. There was the energy of all that power to "keep him in his place." The system itself was calculated to break him even if the overseer failed to do so.

In the marketplace there is a tremendous energy to scramble to the top, to beat back less fortunate individuals, and to step on others in the race to be best. Power! Everyone wants power, and the way to get more power is to exercise it in every decision every step of the way to the top. Sexual power is one way to make a bid for more power. It is also a way to subjugate others to one's already established power. Thus, some persons sleep with others to get to the top; others sleep around so that they can practice the beneficence of the powerful by being generous with their sexuality. It is always a master/slave relationship. This sex has nothing to do with love or even lust. It is the user and the used, and good stories are written when occasionally their roles are reversed and the user becomes the victim, and vice versa.

I see the aggressors in sexual harassment as both victims and predators. The white overseer in "Dave's Necklace" was as much a victim of the system of slavery as Dave. Even before he was fired by the master for his unjust treatment of Dave, he was himself one of the system's greatest victims. So it is with predators. They have characteristics of both, victims and predators.

Characteristics of Sexual Harassers

They Are Victims of:

The system. They have learned that this is the way to behave. It may have happened to them on the way up.

The news and entertainment media. All the information in their environment points to the fact that their behavior is acceptable and estimable.

Their own aggressions and fears. Let's face it, we all have a small reptilian brain buried deep within us. It is only with great effort that we learn to control the emotions connected with this part of our brain. This heritage is part of our human condition.

Other predators and are thus predisposed to hurting others. Child abuse, for one thing,

They Are Predators Because:

They behave as such. They stalk their victims, make them feel powerless and used

They threaten. The consequences of noncompliance are dire: loss of job, failure of a course, court-martial, loss of life.

They act like beasts. They incorporate the rules of the jungle in their dealings with other human beings. They dehumanize the workplace and introduce their own version of "survival of the fittest" into the power game.

They have failed to learn from their own experiences. Instead of becoming more civilized in the face of the leaves lasting imprints, and one may have a real need to exert power to compensate for being preyed upon in youth. The abuse may have been sexual, which would account for a lot of sexual harassment. need to survive, they have reverted to the survival techniques of the jungle. They use power to hurt, humiliate, and abuse others. Sexual harassment thus becomes one way of getting back at all those who have, even symbolically, beaten, castrated, or dehumanized them.

Ted's Views of the Sexual Harasser

Unlike Monica, I do not think the whole clue to the personality of sexual harassers lies in their need for power. I do feel that it certainly has some bearing on their behavior, but I think there is another equally compelling factor, and that is, very simply, lust. There is a great availability of sexual objects, and in my opinion that is how the sexual harasser views sexual partners. They are objects to be lusted after.

Of course, one uses objects, and, as Monica has made clear, if there are users and victims, power must be at issue. I agree that there is an element of the need to control another, even to abase and subjugate, but I believe another basic need is at the root of sexual harassment.

I agree with Monica that no love is involved in these situations, but I do think there is a fair amount of lust. At least, I think sexual harassers are indulging an age-old proclivity for the young and inexperienced as a sexual partner. I think sexual harassers are acting out what they believe to be acceptable behaviors, given the messages they receive from the entertainment media. The media myth is: It is OK to go after the young because only the young are desirable. Only the young have lovely, soft, supple skin. Only the young have lustrous eyes and full, moist lips. Only the young smell good. Only the young are firm yet tender, full-bodied yet sinewy, active yet passive.

Only young women, the myth goes, can give adequate pleasure to men because they haven't been sexually active long enough to lose the elasticity and tightness of their vaginal muscles. Hence the everlasting need to search out girls young enough to be good in bed but not young enough to be "jail bait."

The problem today is that more and more youngsters are becoming sexually active much younger. It is harder and harder to find one who hasn't "given it away" already, probably years ago. It is harder and harder to find partners with whom one can be "the first." Youngsters are either choosing other juveniles as partners or are being victimized earlier. By the time a teenager is old enough for that first job, most co-workers or managers probably assume that the young girl has been on the pill and sexually active for years, and that the young boy has been experienced in sex for a long time. What difference, the conclusion might be, would another sexual liaison make to her or to him?

Only young men have the strength and staying power for really good sex, the myth informs us. They are at the peak of their sexuality, and what good fortune if they can be lured into bed with first-job bonuses dangled before their eyes. Also one is not as likely to get into trouble for seducing a boy as a girl.

Virginity, it seems, has never been an appealing attribute for a boy beyond some undetermined point in his development. It is always expected that young men have learned what they need to know before they get married, even if it means getting their education from older women. Thus, an employer might consider a young man fair game, much more so than a female of the same age. For a young man, sexual education is considered an important "rite of passage" in coming to manhood. This is inherent in the theme of William Faulkner's *The Reivers*, a story about the rite of passage into manhood.

This kind of sexual harassment, which is common on the job and in schools and colleges, is based on lust, I think, and is the result of the presentation of the young as the only desirable sex objects. And as objects they are viewed and treated in this society. They are objects placed on view by the media for our sexual gratification, either homosexual or heterosexual.

Pornography that exploits the young also stems from lust and the view that youth are valuable for sex. Much of the growing problem in the child slave trade, the stealing of children and their sexual abuse, is a result of this same desire to obtain the benefit of someone's virginity.

I believe that *most* sexual harassers are not sick people. They are persons who have been programmed to think and act about sex by the messages that they have received from the media all their lives. I also believe, though, that a significant number of the harassers are really ill, and they are the ones who ultimately become involved in child molesting or child pornography or both.

Like Monica, I believe that these persons may be both victims and perpetrators.

Sexual Harassers as Victims and Perpetrators

Victims	*Perpetrators*
They may have been sexually abused as	They are unwilling to obtain the skills to break

youngsters (or harassed on the job).

They are the victims of a relentless media message that only the young have value as sexual "material." The younger, the better is the obvious conclusion of that premise.

They may view themselves as "sex objects" and have difficulty seeing anyone else as a person separate from his/her sexuality. They are part of a system that rewards macho behavior and deprecates qualities of goodness, loyalty, and virtue as being "weak."

Lust is considered acceptable "good ole boy" or "foxy lady" behavior.

the pattern of behavior.

They are mindless, spineless, and weak. They cannot grow beyond the media myth and message. They act as cruelly and crassly as any Nazi using young girls and boys.

They cannot be excused for not seeking the help and counseling that would free them to become productive human beings. Many such persons regard therapy as something for the "weak" and refuse to change.

They refuse to choose or to learn about role models who are admirable examples of humanity. It is much easier to follow the line of least resistance, and lust is on that line.

Dialogue about the Nature of Harassers

Ted
I see sexual harassers as persons indulging their

Monica
I don't see harassment as "foreplay" at all. I see it as

basic lust. They may not go "all the way" with their victims, but they get their kicks in the "foreplay" stage of harassment.

It is quite titillating for some people to scare others about sexual matters. They consider sex to be better as a result of the "scare."

I agree that it is very sick and often leads to incredible abuse, even perhaps, to death. However, I think people have been given the message in our society that a little harassment goes a long way in spicing up the work-place "ambience."

a vicious, subtle way to say to someone: "Look, I've got control of your life, and you'd better not forget it or you won't last long around here."

Well, if you're talking about the Marquis de Sade, I guess I'll have to agree with you, but if harassment is just another form of using whips and chains, it is very sick and justifies my belief that it is basically about power.

If by "ambience" you mean threats, physical abuse, and sarcasm, that would certainly be more spice than I would care to have dished up to me! I could do with a little more of the milk of human kindness. I feel that this harassment is one of the first steps leading to real violence, rape or even murder.

In the letter from the reader calling himself "Mister Cool," the writer talked about "doing it to" his girl. I consider such an attitude toward sex to be violent and simply an exercise of power.

I agree that to say one is "doing it to" someone when referring to sex is demeaning. I still claim it is a matter of lust, however, a matter of considering the sex partner as an object to whom the act is "done."

What do you say, Readers, after this first column on the issue of sexual harassment? Please write to us.

Ted & Monica

Chapter V

Diary Entry by Young & Alone

Dear Diary:

I hadn't expected to be even more confused after getting so much advice! It's amazing how many different things people can say about just one thing. I'd thought everybody else would be able to give me the answer I wanted. I'm beginning to think that I may have to discover my own solution.

And I certainly hadn't considered that my situation was in any way dangerous. I hadn't even thought about the possibility of physical harm or murder. Some of these letters are really very frightening. Of course, I don't believe that every person who harasses you is a potential rapist or murderer, but how do you know who is and who isn't? It does happen.

The one thing my correspondence through Ted & Monica's column has done for me is make me sure that I am not alone with this problem. Other people have suffered from it, too, and that is conforting to know. Strange that I should feel better just knowing that someone else has suffered. It's not that I wish other people to suffer; it's just that it is so important to me to realize I'm not alone. It's kind of a validation that I'm not crazy.

I can say to myself: "Hey, look! Other people have gone through the same thing, so it can't just be in your imagination. You can't just be making it up. You can't be so confused in your thinking that you see something when nothing is there. It's a shadow, but it's a real shadow, and other people have seen this very real, ugly shadow themselves."

I'm not any closer to a real solution as to how to handle this mess at work. Perhaps, Diary, if I outline some things to you, it will make the possibilities clearer. You remember how it helped me just to confront myself with everything by writing to you the last time. Let me try to focus on the information I have received from Ted & Monica's column and from the letters, both those that were printed in the paper and the ones that Ted & Monica sent to me privately. If I make a list, I may be able to come to some better way of figuring out an answer.

What I've Learned about Sexual Harassment

1. It happens all the time, and people don't talk about it because:
   a. The victim may look as if he/she knows how to handle the situation so they don't say anything to him/her.
   b. They may be too scared of what might happen to them if they started running their mouths off to the victim. They might lose their job or start getting picked on themselves.
   c. Some people might be jealous of the attention the victim is getting.
   d. People don't know that other people go through the same kinds of things, so they keep quiet out of embarrassment or shame.
   e. Some co-workers might think the victim is stupid and they would know what to do about such a situation.
   f. Some might think it's funny, just a big joke.

2. Young persons don't always tell their parents about it because:
   a. They think their parents might make them quit the job.
   b. They think their parents might make things worse by creating trouble.
   c. They think their co-workers might find out about their parents' intervening for them, and that would be embarrassing.
   d. Some parents would be shocked to think such things could happen and might not even believe their child.
3. Counseling might help because:
   a. It can give you a better perspective on things.
   b. You can get advice from someone who has much more experience and who has helped other people.
   c. A counselor won't think you're stupid.
   d. A counselor won't create embarrassing situations for you at work.
   e. A counselor will help you see how to help yourself.
4. Some people don't even see that this could be a problem because:
   a. "All young people" are supposed to have had a lot of sex by the time they are ready to go out into the world to make a living. Teenagers are expected to know how to take care of themselves.
   b. Sexual harassment is just "innocent" fun, a sort of harmless teasing that doesn't mean anything.
   c. You get what you ask for, and if you dress or act in a sexually precocious way, people will assume you are very experienced in matters of sex.
5. Sexual harassment can be very serious because:

a. It can lead to violence such as rape or murder.
b. Even if other violent actions do not occur, the victim may be forced to change his/her whole life as a result of this relationship. The victim may enter into a relationship (heterosexual or homosexual) that is difficult to get out of.
c. Other careers and education may be interrupted or never completed because of this relationship. The other person may have such control over the victim's life that the victim loses sight of any other goals.

6. Dealing with sexual harassment effectively is an art because:
   a. The consequences can be so serious.
   b. Some people seem to have instinctive skills in handling such situations.
   c. Many people seem to be at a loss about handling themselves in such situations.

7. Views of the sexual harasser:
   a. He or she may just be indulging lust, especially for the young.
   b. The harasser may be into power, with a lot of hatred and violence in his/her character.
   c. The harasser may be a harmless jerk conditioned by this environment to think sexual harassment is funny.

And so, Dear Diary, that is it in a nutshell. Those are the insights into sexual harassment I've received so far. I've still not got the answer, Dear Diary. I still don't know what to do. But I can see the problem a little better, if that makes any sense to you. I'll bet you're thinking, Diary, that we were supposed to be looking for the solution, not trying to see the problem more clearly. Well, I feel like Indiana Jones in "Raiders of the Lost Ark." Do you remember how, at the beginning of the movie, Indiana was searching for the gold figure in the cave? There were all sorts of horrors and traps along the passage to the interior of the cave where the treasure was. Indiana had to be able to see every trap before he could even begin to solve the problem of getting the gold figure. That's how I feel right now, like Indiana Jones, and you, Dear Diary, are my faithful companion who can help me by letting me see things along the way. If I don't see the traps, I'll never get the treasure, which is: the solution to my problem. Here are the traps as I see them. Help me where you can, Diary.

Traps in the Problem of Sexual Harassment

Trap 1. I'm not sure of myself. I'm not secure enough with myself to deal with all the feelings involved in this situation.

Trap 2. I'm not sure whether my boss is a jerk, a lecher, or a violent person full of hatred.

Trap 3. I'm not sure how my parents might react.

Trap 4. I don't know whom to go to for counseling.

Now, Diary, let's investigate each of those traps a little more closely. I'll feed you the information, and you give me some of your usual brilliant feedback. We'll do it this way. I'll list feelings I have that correspond to each *Trap*. On a scale of 1 to 5 I'll rate my feelings. We'll do *Trap* 1 first. This is how I feel about my own qualities. I'll list some things that are important to me.

Bad Vibrations 1=20%	*Some Good, Some Bad Vibes* 2=40%	*Uncertain How I Feel* 3=60%	*Pretty Good* 4=80%	*100% Positive* 5=100%

A. Self-confidence—3
B. Sexuality—4

C. Independence—2 (I thought I had it till I got this job!)
D. Sense of Humor—4
E. Self-motivation—4 (always good grades, etc.)
F. Responsibility—4
G. Sensitivity—2 (for others, but for myself, too)
H. Outgoingness—4
I. Trust—3
J. Patience—1

That adds up to a score of 31 out of a possible 50 points, or 62 percent if I divide 31 by 50. That means that my feelings about myself are in the category of *Uncertain*.

Now, if I use the same chart for *Trap* 2, I may find out how I feel about my boss. My boss is:

A. Attractive—2 (not bad-looking, just a yukky person)
B. Uncomfortable to Be Around—1
C. Fair—2
D. Patient—2
E. Sense of Humor—1 (I do not get good vibes here!)
F. Trustworthy—1
G. Likable—2
H. Sensitive—1
I. Outgoing—2 (talks a lot, but not very open)
J. Violent—3

My boss scores 17 out of a possible 50, or, dividing 50 by 17, 34 percent. That puts him/her somewhere between absolutely bad vibrations and a mix of good/bad vibes. That's just about accurate, too. There are things about my boss that I don't like at all, but I think he/she does some things fairly well. I know the cash is always taken care of; the place seems clean and in good order. I can't complain about everything!

How do I feel about my parents? Let's do *Trap* 3.

A. Trusting—5
B. Loving—4
C. Considerate—4 (usually)
D. Patient—2 (they aren't *perfect!*)
E. Happy—4
F. Strict—2 (*very!*)
G. Sense of Humor—4
H. Fair—4
I. Sensitive—4
J. Tolerant—3 (I just don't know about this one!)

My parents rate 36 out of a possible 50, or a good 72 percent if I divide 36 by 50. That's not bad, Diary. According to my chart, that means my parents are almost *Pretty good*! Maybe I ought to trust my parents more and talk to them about this. I'm not going to do the chart on a counselor, because I don't know a counselor to go to yet!

Now I'm going to do something, Diary, that will help me see if this job is really worth all the hassle. I'm going to put possible considerations about the job in two columns, one called *Rewarding*, and the other *Demeaning*. There are definitely some things about any job that ought to be rewarding. Right? And in my situation, there are certainly some things that are demeaning, which make me feel less than a person.

Rewarding	*Demeaning*
Making money	Feeling threatened
Becoming more independent	Fear
Making new friends	Shame
Learning things	Feeling alone
Gaining experience	Uncertainty
Learning to deal with difficulties	Indecision

Being successful   Feeling manipulated
Being looked up to by peers   Feeling naive
Establishing new goals   Confusion
Growing   Fear of failure

As I look across each pair I am going to underline the item from each column that best fits my present situation. When I have finished I ought to have a fair idea whether this job, staying on and working at this place for this boss, is worth all the pain it causes me. If I have underlined more things from the *Demeaning* column, I ought to have my answer, shouldn't I, Diary? Then I need to decide what to do.

Chapter VI

Stacy's Story—Letter to Ted & Monica

Dear Ted & Monica:

Please pass this letter on to Young & Alone. I really don't want you to print it in the paper, but when I saw that letter from Young & Alone I knew I just had to do something to help. The things that happen in life, even the bad things, can have meaning if we can help someone else by what we know, don't you agree? Let's just say I am someone very close to Stacy (not her real name), and I have suffered a lot because of her actions.

When Stacy went to work at Wendy's she was fifteen years old. It was the summer between her sophomore and junior years at Rockland High School, and the next two years should have been the most wonderful of her life. Even though she was the youngest member of her class, she was among those who seemed to have the most promise for the future.

Stacy was to be the co-editor of the school paper in her junior year and would certainly be the editor in her senior year. She planned on taking off a week from her new job that summer so that she could attend a journalism camp with the newspaper sponsor and three other student staffers.

She was in the French Club, a member of the Student Council, and in the National Honor Society. She took all Advanced Program classes at school. Easily among the top ten percent of her class, she looked forward to scholarships, college bids, and a career in microbiology. Already she had been voted—first by her homeroom, and then by all her classmates—to be in the football homecoming court during her freshman and sophomore years.

Stacy was one of the prettiest and most popular girls at Rockland High. She was five feet three and weighed 113 pounds. Her dark brown hair, which came just below her shoulders, had enough natural curl in it for wonderful body. She wore it just tucked under at the edges for a slight page-boy effect. Stacy had spectacular eyes; her unmascaraed lashes were thick and long and curled upward from dark brown eyes.

Still, it wasn't just her natural beauty that endeared her to everyone at school. There was a sweetness about Stacy. She had a way of making everyone else feel special. Whether this was artifice or not, no one ever knew. Stacy had entered high school knowing how to talk to people, how to listen to them, and how to get them to listen to her. She could manipulate teachers and students alike with the ease of a United States Senator charming the hometown folks at a 4th of July picnic.

You could see Stacy at just about every home game the school played, and that wasn't restricted to football. Even during the spring sports season, Stacy came and cheered the baseball team, the tennis team, the golf team. Although sports didn't seem to interest her enough to try out for any team herself, she did enjoy the boys' sports activities and was one of the most faithful fans at the school. And there was always a crowd of young men around her at the games. Stacy had plenty of dates and went with several guys during her first two years of high school.

Her job at Wendy's interfered a little with her social life. Several times each week she had to work the late shift, and even though the restaurant closed at eleven, she was there until twelve-thirty or one in the morning cleaning up. The job interfered with her social life in more significant ways than that, however. It wasn't very long until Stacy no longer shared the kind of social life that the majority of her friends at school did.

At the very first Wendy's where Stacy worked, Allyson was one of her bosses. Allyson was not Stacy's immediate supervisor; she was the supervisor for four restaurants in the chain. Allyson began, however, to spend considerably more time in this restaurant, and she always managed to be around when Stacy got off late. By the time school started again in late summer, Stacy had a whole new set of goals, and it wasn't long before the change in her became noticeable to her friends and teachers. Stacy's family had been quite uncomfortable about it for some time.

At first Stacy's mother had been grateful for Allyson's kindness to her daughter. She had met Allyson and had had the young woman over for dinner a few times during the summer, as Stacy seemed so fond of her. Allyson was twenty-two and seemed like a very level-headed person, intent on becoming a manager of a Wendy's restaurant. It had been a relief to the mother to have someone she could trust pick Stacy up after work. She and Stacy's father both had to get up early for work (she was a psychologist, he was an investment banker), and they did not relish having to stay up till one-thirty to bring Stacy home. Until Allyson made the offer, Stacy's father had usually been the one to get her.

It must have been Stacy's younger brother who first alerted the mother that something was wrong. At any rate, the mother heard him teasing Stacy about coming home around daylight and coming home drunk. When she and her husband tried to talk to Stacy about it, the girl accused her brother of lying, of making up stories, and of trying to cause trouble. In the meantime, Stacy still went over to the neighborhood pool to swim and sun herself during the days, but she seemed less and less involved with any youngsters her own age. Her mother was glad when school started and she could get Stacy to change her schedule. There was no way Stacy could work the late shift and keep up with her Advanced Program at school. Stacy, however, would not hear of changing her schedule at Wendy's, and when her mother tried to talk to her boss about it, Stacy got really ugly and told her to mind her own business.

The parents then decided to pick Stacy up themselves when she worked the late shift. It was at this point that things became frantic. If Stacy was working late, Allyson was always around. Either she was in the restaurant waiting for Stacy or in her car in the parking lot. The mother could not force Stacy into her car; Stacy sneaked off the lot with Allyson if the father came to get her. She simply would not go home with her parents and always left with Allyson.

The mother tried going to Wendy's earlier in the evening to talk to Stacy on her breaks. If Stacy decided to take her break while her mother was there, she sat with her and refused to discuss the situation about Allyson. Usually she refused to take her breaks if her mother was in the restaurant, even though her mother sometimes sat for over an hour just to get a chance to talk to her. Her mother was worried about what was happening to her daughter. Even the school counselor had called her about the sudden drop in Stacy's grades.

By the end of her junior year, Stacy was a much different person. All she ever talked about was her job at Wendy's and the career advantages for her there. She did not apply for scholarships, and she gave up considering microbiology as a career. She dropped from eighth in her class to thirty-seventh, she no longer attended school functions, and she rarely had dates. Her work on the school paper suffered, but because she had received so much editorial training the sponsor still wanted her to be the editor during her senior year.

Stacy's senior year was a disaster. The first major catastrophe happened on her seventeenth birthday early in the fall. The sponsor of the paper baked a birthday cake for Stacy, and the staff had chipped in to buy her a T-shirt. The school paper staff met during fifth period, toward the end of the school day.

Stacy informed the sponsor that she would have to leave early that day, that she had an appointment with managers of Wendy's to discuss her enrollment in a managerial training course in the spring. Allyson was to pick her up. The teacher was so disappointed that she told Stacy about the party, which was to have been a surprise. Stacy seemed genuinely touched, but explained that she really had no choice; she had obtained permission from her counselor to leave, and she simply must keep the appointment. Her future depended on it. She took her T-shirt and left.

Stacy left school with Allyson around lunch time. She did not return home that night, and her parents frantically called teachers to find out what had happened. Stacy did not come to school at all on the following day, but she did finally call her mother to say that she was fine and with Allyson. When she did return to school she was wearing a new T-shirt, one that Allyson had given her for her birthday. The words on the back of the shirt were "SOFT 'N' SWEET."

Stacy had friends at school who had been close to her for a long time; they openly professed concern over her now. They had been aware for some time that something very strange was happening in Stacy's life. Whenever they had gone to Wendy's for lunch and to chat for a minute with Stacy, Allyson would move right over to that spot and pretend to be very busy doing something. She often stood right behind Stacy and glowered at them. The kids stopped coming around to see Stacy. They stopped bothering with her at all.

Stacy began a pattern of coming to school too late for first or second period and leaving after fourth period. She only needed a few credits to graduate and had to be there for her senior English class. Her grades in the Advanced Program English were so bad after the first grading period that she had to be assigned to an easier English class, which she barely managed to pass. She gave up the idea of college altogether; her only ambition was to become manager of a Wendy's restaurant.

Her life at home became traumatic. One day when her parents were out of the house Stacy packed all her belongings and moved into Allyson's apartment. The parents were broken-hearted. The school counselor suggested the possibility of taking legal action to get Stacy back, but they felt that would simply alienate her all the more. They feared that if they made trouble at Wendy's either Allyson or Stacy would lose her job, and that would make Stacy hate them forever. They tried to keep in touch with her by notes, visiting her at Wendy's, and giving her brother messages for her at school.

The burden on her brother was too heavy. He was a freshman at Rockland High. The upperclassmen were always asking him questions about Stacy or making crude remarks about her relationship with Allyson. He began to fail classes, then to cut school for days at a time. The next year he transferred to a different school.

When Stacy came to school she drove Allyson's car. Allyson bought her new clothes. Stacy drank heavily and often had such a hangover that she could not function in class at all. Allyson maintained a tight control over her life, but Stacy said that she and Allyson were just "good friends." She explained her need to get away from home and established Allyson as the savior who had rescued her from her unhappy home life. Allyson had promised to get her promotions and introduced her to all kinds of job opportunities at Wendy's, she said.

Stacy declined a nomination for basketball homecoming; she did not go to that game or the dance afterward, and she refused all dates. Although she told everyone about a wonderful fellow she had met at Wendy's who was taking her to the senior prom, she never showed up at the dance. She had described her dress at length to her friends and had even made plans to join a group of them at a restaurant for dinner before the prom. She could not even be reached on the night of the prom.

The school paper limped along without a qualified editor for the rest of the year. Stacy avoided the sponsor as much as she could until the sponsor found an occasion to confront her and tell her that she would always be welcome in the newspaper room and that there were no hard feelings.

By the end of her senior year, Stacy no longer tried to hide the fact that she and Allyson were lovers. They were seen in public more often, holding hands, giggling, or kissing. Stacy's close friends still tried to be friendly to her, but she closed off any attempt at friendliness from anyone but Allyson. She rarely visited her parents' home, and when she did go she was usually drunk and fought with them. Her brother wouldn't speak to her.

Stacy did not go on to become manager of a Wendy's restaurant. Within two years of graduation from high school, she had quit Wendy's. She spent long periods out of work before going from job to job in other fast-food chains.

Her parents kept in touch with Stacy, however. They

invited her for Thanksgiving and Christmas. They were there when she was broke. Little by little she began coming to the house more often. Once she fell asleep on the bed in her old room. Then she stayed for a weekend and moved a few of her things back.

It was all over by the time Stacy was twenty-one. She came to her parents crying and explained that Allyson had put her out for a new lover, a younger girl working at Wendy's. Eventually Allyson lost her job at Wendy's; someone finally reported her and got her in trouble. But she had done a lot of mischief in the meantime. And she never really lost her control over Stacy. She could get Stacy into an emotional frenzy even after she had thrown her over for a new lover. There never was a clean break for Stacy, not even after she had moved back home.

And for the first time Stacy's parents heard the full story of how much that job had meant to their daughter when she was fifteen—so much, in fact, that she had been willing to accept Allyson's advances to keep the job. She had been promised that she could become a "crew chief" at first. A crew chief is just under the assistant manager. If you get to be a crew chief, the chances are pretty good that you'll be put into management-training. Stacy wanted to become a crew chief, an assistant manager, and a manager-trainee more than anything in the world. Somehow this job had gobbled up all her other goals and her whole life, too.

Then, too, she enjoyed the attention she got from the relationship. Granted, some of it was pretty negative attention. Everyone was whispering and giggling about Stacy, calling her a lesbian. In the beginning that seemed just to make her more defiant and set in her new ways. She was like someone daring the world to challenge her. It was kind of "in" to be involved in a relationship like this, if you know what I mean.

Finally, she was in so deep and had changed her life so significantly that she had to keep going in the new direction. It wasn't so exciting when there wasn't any challenge to it anymore. She had entered a way of life that kept her, after her graduation from high school, from seeing any of her old friends or getting involved in the things that interested them. They were either working, away at college, or married. They had passed Stacy by and only referred to her at the occasional lunch or get-together when someone might ask: "By the way, whatever happened to Stacy?" Hardly anyone ever knew.

With the challenge gone out of her relationship with Allyson, things took on a new light for Stacy. Much of the tension, the excitement, had gone from her life, too. She was too old for her parents to take legal action for her return home. Her brother joined the Marines and didn't care anymore what Stacy did with her life. Her social life became confined to friends who shared interests and goals with her and Allyson. Stacy's naturally curious and creative mind stagnated from the lack of challenge that college could have provided. She found, by age twenty-one, that the pursuit of success in a fast-food chain was not everything she had dreamed it would be when she was fifteen. She had let a lot of wonderful opportunities go by. She wasn't even sure she could get into a college now; she had barely graduated from high school and had dropped to the bottom of her senior class.

Well, Ted & Monica, I'll end my letter about Stacy there. I hope you will see that Young & Alone gets it. This was a wonderful girl who was so eager to get ahead in her first job. That job meant everything to her, and when Allyson offered the chance for advancement, she did whatever Allyson wanted.

Sometimes this happens to young people who are too

eager and who want to get ahead the fastest way possible. Others are just slow workers, and they are the ones who might be easy prey to unscrupulous bosses, especially if they are really anxious to keep their job. The slow ones—the ones who work in fast-food places and can't keep up the pace, can't make change fast, can't get the food out fast, can't take the orders and fill them quickly—they're the ones who are vulnerable to exploitation. Someone says to them: "I'll overlook that you're so slow if you'll just——."

Stacy is dead now. She had spent too many years drinking heavily and living her life to please someone else. When Allyson rejected her, she couldn't put her life back together. Her parents tried; so did counselors. She was too filled with discouragement over all that she had given up, too frightened of all that she would have to do to make a new start. She shot herself.

A Mourner for Stacy

Chapter VII

Who Are Victims of Sexual Harassment? Ted & Monica's Column

Dear Readers:

In our last column we discussed "Who Is the Sexual Harasser?" Today we want to present what information we have on the persons who become victims of sexual harassment. We have concluded from our research that it is much more common than most people think. For a long time it was simply endured by its victims, mostly women, as another painful reminder of their obvious position of subservience in a male-dominated society. In other words, if you were already a second-class citizen by virtue of your birth as a female, you should not be surprised at being further diminished in your humanity when you entered the work force, matriculated at college, or joined the armed services.

You had no rights that could be violated if you were a woman. You could not, like Jacob, trick the management into thinking you were your brother Esau and so secure your birthright, your heritage as a human being. You could not, again like Jacob, wrestle with the angel for a new name, a name that would carry the weight, significance, and power of the *chosen* in this world where you were always an alien, an other, lesser being. You were like Benjamin, violated by your brothers and cast out.

But Benjamin rose to a position of great power in

Egypt. He murdered one man, but he forgave his brothers and showed them a bold generosity of spirit. Women have occasionally done as was done unto them when they became powerful. They have occasionally been as ruthless as men once they rose to power. They have occasionally victimized others and been harassers for sexual favors also.

In this modern world where curious exhibitions of some kind of equality often exist, both men and women may be victims or harassers. In our complex society, heterosexual men and women as well as homosexual men and women may be either victims or abusers. Sexual harassment usually occurs when someone has some kind of power of persuasion over someone else, some reason that makes it important for the victim to comply. The harassers may well have been victims at some time. They are surely victims of a society that considers success in terms of failure, that measures winning in the context of losing, and that rates achievers on a spiral with losers at the bottom. There is often a lack of generosity of spirit in those climbing to the top of this spiral, and the achievers of this kind of success, men or women, may have trodden on others to get there.

It is time we took a look at these victims, the victims of a particular form of abuse—sexual harassment. We shall begin by trying to establish just what it is that the victim has to gain by cooperating with the harassment, by allowing himself/herself to continue to be abused. And we shall try to determine what the victim loses by participation in the contest of sexual harassment. In other words, what's in it for the victim? It is necessary to understand the answers to this basic question if we are to find out more about the character of victims. We cannot find out who they are until we know why they play the game in the first place. And they are involved in a game, albeit a dangerous and perverse one.

The following is a list of considerations that hold out promise of reward for the victim of sexual harassment. These seven goodies seem to be what the victim thinks will ensure success for him/her. They are the *seven capital signs* of reward for the victim.

The Seven Capital Signs

1. Job Security—He/she may see this as the only way to keep a job and the money that goes with it.
2. Promotion—In the victim's eyes this may be the fastest, or the only, way to the top.
3. Recommendations—That résumé may appear awfully important to the victim.
4. Attention—This kind of attention may be entirely new to the victim.
5. Reduction of Conflict—Some people would do anything to avoid scenes and unpleasantness.
6. Acceptance—The victim may actually see this as a form of being told: "I like you."
7. Status—The victim may think this is a singular situation and worthy of some distinction.

Each of these seven capital signs, you will notice, confers something on the victim. No one of them originates from within the victim as a form of inner strength, nor is any one of them even an interior goal to be achieved. Instead of viewing these goals as intrinsic rewards for adequate performance on the job, in class, or on base, the victim believes cooperation with the aggressor to be the better route to success. The seven capital signs are gifts that the victim thinks will be bestowed upon him/her for playing along with the harasser. The goodies will come from the outside, from the aggressor. As such, the victim is totally at the mercy of the aggressor to obtain the goodies.

These rewards, like a mantle from the king, will confer upon the person of Cinderella or Cinderfella a royal status in the realm of the workplace, school, college, or military base. Who knows, the mantle may extend beyond the obvious limits and confer upon the wearer a means of obtaining triumph elsewhere. The mantle may actually validate the victim's existence.

If these seven capital signs are benefits to be bestowed by the harasser, what are the characteristics of the potential victim? Who is the person when stripped of the mantle? In other words, what does the victim already bring to the game? Whether stud poker or marbles, no one enters into play unless the opponent brings along the materials for the game. Neither will the aggressor enter into play if the opponent/victim comes without the necessary raw materials for victimization.

That may seem unfair. The woman in Charlotte Perkins Gilman's story "The Yellow Wallpaper" can hardly be discredited for bringing all her marbles into the game—and losing them. She went stark, raving mad. She entered into the yellow wallpaper and became part of the pattern. She tore the paper from the wall in shreds and hunks and crawled around the room in which she was a virtual prisoner babbling incoherencies.

She had been kept there by her husband, a "kind and sympathetic" man who cared only about her cure from a case of "nerves." When she begged to be allowed to visit friends, he refused, claiming that it would be too exerting for her. When she heard his step on the stairs, when she heard him coming with her tray of food, she hid the writing she was doing, knowing that he would not approve of her creative exercises. Her creativity became madness. Her "kind and sympathetic" husband seemed stunned at her loss of humanity.

It may be unfair to designate one of the soldiers in Guy de Maupassant's "Two Little Soldiers" as coming into the drama with all the attributes that led to his loss of life by—suicide. He was loyal, generous, kind, affectionate, open-hearted. He was a good man, and his best friend and the girl he loved made a fool of him and laughed at his love.

The young man who became the real victim in Richard Connell's "The Most Dangerous Game" was himself a predator. He simply was not as good at it as the man who stalked him.

It is often said that there are some people who will never be victims. The corollary to this statement may then be: There are some people who will always be victims. Who are these people, and what is it they have (or do not have) that denotes them as losers?

Are they simply those who have been programmed to fail since birth, those wretched souls who have never gained love and acceptance in their families? Are they the girls whose mothers contended against them as tiny babies, determined that no girl-child would take their husband from them? Are they the boys whose father browbeat them into exhibiting the manly characteristics they knew they lacked? Are the victims and losers as easy to spot as the characters in a Greek play where one reads among the tragedies of Antigone, Medusa, Orestes, Clytemnestra, and the others the tragedy of one's own life? What is the interior proclivity to being victimized that one brings to the drama of life?

We shall examine, then, this propensity for victimization in the light of the following list, the self-defeating dozen.

What the Victim Brings to the Game of Harassment:
The Self-defeating Dozen

1. Misplaced trust—The victim may never have been able to trust anyone before, or may have led a life

where everyone was trusted; thus no distinction is made between individuals.

2. Lack of confidence—The victim may never have had any success before the singular accomplishment of landing this job.

3. Fear of failure—The victim may have realized acute failure prior to this job, or may feel that everything attempted has resulted in dreary failure. The victim may desperately need not to fail at this job because of having to support self and others.

4. Sense of inadequacy—The adage, "Don't do anything unless you can do it right," may have been hammered into this person so deeply that he/she is paralyzed with fear in performing any duty.

5. Poor self-image—The victim may feel like a loser.

6. Guilelessness—The victim is a good person and expects everyone else to be good, too. The Big Bad Wolf exists only in fairy tales.

7. Gullibility—"What big eyes you have, Grandmother!"

8. Greed—It is said that there is a little larceny in all of us, and that it is merely a question of finding what it is we will sell out for. There could be no "pigeon-drops" without people willing to be seduced by con artists who offer huge sums to "match" the victim's "investment." The victim has to want what the harasser has to offer. A promotion that one does not deserve may seem like a good "carrot" to reach for.

9. Egotism—"I am the one who won the attentions of this person. Therefore, I must be somebody!"

10. Possessiveness—"What I've earned (however dubiously), I'm going to keep for myself."

11. Lack of creativity—The victim lacks humor or

other imaginative capabilities by which he/she could defuse the situation.

12. Inexperience—This condition, which is experienced by all persons at some time in their lives, may be the one that causes the predator to sniff the victim out. Even if the victim is self-assured and confident, the fact of inexperience makes him/her vulnerable. In every new situation a person becomes vulnerable again, and that vulnerability alone may be enough to attract predators. Thus, even saints are tempted, and the good must also learn to resist evil.

These are the *self-defeating dozen* that we have come up with as a result of our research. To some extent it is the presence of one or more of these sources of vulnerability that makes victims fall prey to aggressors. The list actually offers a catalog of those things in us that accompany vulnerability and may perhaps be said to be the cause of it.

We shall have more to say about these dozen weakening characteristics in a later column. However, as was the case with our column on the sexual harasser, we have some differing views on the effects of these twelve character traits in the victim. We present our views for you here and let you be the judge.

Ted's Opinion
It is important to recall here that Sigmund Freud, as a result of his studies, concluded that there is incredible "garbage" in us human beings, that we are capable of the vilest deeds

Monica's Opinion
Perhaps we would do better to recall Carl Jung's belief that the weakness and evil we find in ourselves belong to the "shadow" side of our selves, and that if there is shadow, there

and only refrain from doing those deeds because of the powerful superego. We do not publish this list of the *self-defeating dozen* to discourage or dismay you, but to shed some light on those traits that we all share by virtue of our humanity.

I mean that, in very subtle ways, the victim is an accomplice in his/her own destruction. No one is totally innocent. In his book *The Book*, Alan Watts brought out the fact that evil needs good in order to exist, just as good needs evil. The strong need the weak; light needs darkness. You cannot have one without the other. You cannot have a crime without a victim, and certain beings present themselves as excellent subjects for victimization.

must also be present a very bright light. Surely you can't mean to suggest that the victim is somehow responsible for the attacks against him/her? Surely you don't mean that because the victim is not a perfect person, attack is more likely?

Such as babies and helpless animals? I know of babies who are burned to death; I know of a boy who liked to put puppies in trash cans, pour kerosene on them and set them afire. I knew someone who put a cat inside the hubcap of a car and then went as fast as possible to hear the cat scream in terror. I can think of whole nations of people who have been tyrannized simply because they existed. You aren't going to tell me that they all cooperated with the murderers who destroyed them?

I think, in the case of sexual harassment particularly, that very often the victim sets himself/herself up for it by not being aware of his/her own propensity toward weakness. I think the vulnerability, the shadow side, if you will, within the potential victim elicits a response from the harasser that leads to the victimization. The list of the self-defeating dozen is meant to help people understand themselves so well that they will never elicit an aggressive response from would-be predators.

Camille Saint-Saëns composed a tone poem called "The Youth of Hercules" about the choice Hercules had to make: a life of pleasure or a life of virtue and goodness. Hercules made the choice that led to immortality. You are suggesting that people should know themselves so well that they can make the choices they want in a situation and not be subject to another's determination of how they will act?

Then they wouldn't become victims. At least, they wouldn't participate in the game of "victimization" without full knowledge and full consent.

Ted & Monica

Chapter VIII

Readers' Responses to Ted & Monica

Dear Ted & Monica:

Please print this letter so that someone else may be helped. After I read Young & Alone's story, I knew I had to talk about my case. I've kept it in for so many years and caused a lot of people grief. My story happened when I was in middle school, however.

I'm beginning to think you aren't safe anywhere. I know that there are many good teachers who wouldn't think of going after their students. I just happened to meet up with one who did. The more I have talked to people in later years, the more common I suspect sexual harassment is in the schools, particularly in high schools. I'll bet, on an average, there is one harasser for every high school in a large system. That doesn't mean I think there is a harasser in every single school. Some schools probably don't have any faculty members who would do that. They are lucky, that's all. I know of one faculty in my neighborhood with three persons who have harassed girls or boys.

I met Mr. X when I was in eighth grade. He was the choral director at the nearby high school, and his contract required him to give one class per day at the middle school. I was in the chorus, a soprano who fancied myself a "coloratura." I easily caught the eye as well as the ear of Mr. X, and I flirted with him outrageously.

It was during that year that we started to go out,

although we didn't have sex until I was a freshman. By the end of my freshman year I turned sixteen, so I guess he thought he was safe with me. When I was still in eighth grade we did a lot of other things, but we didn't come right out and "do it." I was crazy about him, and I never would have told on him anyway.

One day during my freshman year (I was at the high school where he spent most of the day), he took me out during his planning period, which was sixth period at the end of the day. He had some errand to run, and he took me along. I cut my class and didn't tell anyone where I was going. When we came back, school was out and we thought we were "safe." He got me in the back seat of his car in the school parking lot. We didn't do very much, because one of my teachers came out of the building and saw us. Well, she went to the principal and raised all kinds of cain.

Mr. X went to the principal, and they laughed and joked about it. The principal was a buddy of Mr. X and let him get away with just about anything. The teacher who had seen us talked to me, and I denied everything; I said my milkshake had fallen back there and we were trying to clean it up. Everybody in the school joked about that teacher and said she was nuts for having tried to cause trouble. It looked like she had lied or was just a trouble-maker.

Anyway, by the time I was a senior things were pretty serious between Mr. X and me. We went out all the time. I would tell my parents I was going over to a friend's house and I would go somewhere with Mr. X. All my friends covered for me with my family. Everybody thought Mr. X was so great. I was the envy of everyone because he was really a hunk! I really worried when other girls flirted with him. I was so jealous of him sometimes that I almost went crazy. The principal knew what was going on, and he would call and talk to me a lot just to see if I was OK. I felt like I was really special!

I began to cut more and more classes and got away with it. The principal let me be his aide one period, and I did typing for him in his office. I think he was trying to keep an eye on me; I think he was worried about me and Mr. X but didn't know what to do about it. He thought, I guess, that he was doing his duty by me if he just looked out for me and saw that I was doing all right, that I was going to make it to graduation.

If I was jealous of Mr. X, he certainly was jealous of me. I couldn't go out with anyone else during my whole high school. I could only go out in a group, and even then he might show up wherever we were just to check up on me. I couldn't even go to my junior and senior proms—not with a date anyway. I managed to go in a group with the losers, all the kids who don't have dates and go to their proms alone. Sometimes they wind up renting a limo and going as a group. My prom nights were terrible. I was so proud of being Mr. X's "steady," yet I couldn't show it off in front of my teachers and classmates. I was miserable.

I was even more miserable when I learned that Mr. X wasn't faithful to me, had never been faithful to me. I met some people who had been students in the last school where he'd taught. "Oh, he always ran around with the girls in that school," they told me. "He's always had his pick of the chicks!"

Mr. X promised to marry me. He was always talking about our getting married, but I might not see him for weeks at a time. Sometimes he'd put me off at school, say he was too busy to talk to me. And then I might not see him at night for weeks and weeks. I found out about all the other women he was dating. I'd call him at home and cry and carry on. Then he might come around and promise me we were getting married right after I graduated. He started coming by my house real late on weekends to see if I was there, but he wouldn't take me out; he'd just demand to know where I was when my parents answered the door.

My parents started to question all this. They started asking me what was going on. I think my mother suspected how deeply I was involved with Mr. X, but neither she nor my dad wanted to believe it.

Then, the summer after graduation, Mr. X's mother died. I was all full of sorrow and sympathy for him. This was the man who wanted to marry me and his mother had just died. I thought about sending flowers, and I was going to go to the funeral parlor and be by his side through the whole thing. I even thought I would probably sit with him in church during the funeral and maybe sing a solo, a hymn for his mother. I would stand weeping next to him in the cemetery, holding his hand at the graveside.

When I called him and finally reached him, he ordered me not even to come to the funeral parlor. He didn't want me at the funeral parlor! He didn't want me at the church! He didn't want me at the cemetery!

It was at this time that my mother got it all out of me. She told me: "Of course, he doesn't want you at his mother's funeral. He has only been using you all along, and now he doesn't want you there for all his friends to see!" I knew she was right.

I had given up my chances for college because I thought he was going to marry me. I had flunked a lot of classes and cut a lot more. My grades, even in the classes I passed, were terrible. I was never going to be a coloratura anything, just a fool. I really fell apart for a few weeks. My father finally persuaded me to move to New York state, where his sister lived. I could get a job there.

Fortunately I wasn't pregnant. Mr. X took great precautions with his women to see that they didn't get pregnant, I guess. Anyway, I've never heard of any babies of his around town.

When I look back, I try to see how I got into this in the first place. I know it started out as a great fun thing, something I had that nobody else in my class had. Then I became totally dependent on him. When I think now of all the fun I missed because he was my "one and only"!

But I've also found out some other things. I told a teacher friend the whole thing sometime ago. She looked kind of funny for a minute, then she told me that everything now made sense.

She had known Mr. X pretty well for several years. He knew she thought a lot of me, and I guess he tried to find out from her, in his devious little ways, how much I might have told her. She said he always talked about me as if he were so worried about me. He told her how my parents didn't care about me, how they neglected me and were never there for me. None of this was true, you see, it's just what he made up to justify his attention to me. This teacher said that even the school counselor thought Mr. X's relationship with me was so wonderful. "At least he's always there for her; that's more than I can say for her family," the counselor told my teacher friend.

I wonder if he really believed that lie he told about my parents? I wonder how many other lies he made up about me to justify his behavior? I wonder what school would have been like for me if I'd lived it more like other girls? I wonder what my life would have been like if I'd gone to college then instead of waiting several more years? Fortunately, my life has turned out fine, no thanks to Mr. X.

Almost a Coloratura

Dear Young & Alone:

I'm sending this letter to Ted & Monica's column hoping that they will print it and you will see it. Sexual harassment happens in schools, too, you know. It happens to boys as well as to girls.

In my school someone walked in on one of our sexiest-looking female teachers. They walked in on her kissing one of her male students in an empty classroom.

This teacher wears tight sweaters and tight jeans to school, and she really knows how to "swing it." The kids call her "Miss Wiggle." The guys all try to get in her classes (and in her jeans), especially now that they know she will give more than grades to her students. The girls hate her; they're all jealous of her.

Did she get punished for kissing a student in school? I don't think so; nobody seems to think so. She did take a three-day "vacation" about that time, but when she came back she said she'd had the flu.

Sexually Harassed Fellow

Dear Young & Alone:

At our school we have a teacher who has a case coming up in court involving child pornography. He is supposed to have used a student for child porn pictures in another school where he taught. They can't fire him until he is proven guilty in court.

We had another teacher who got a girl pregnant this year. He was fired.

We had another teacher who would go to a girl's class, call her out into the hall, and try to make dates with her. She finally got her mother to come to school and do something about it. He isn't around anymore, but I know he hasn't been fired; he's just "somewhere else."

So you see, we've got our full share of these losers in our high school. Three of them (as far as I know)!

Three Strikes and You're Out

Dear Young & Alone:

There was a coach at our school who had sex with girls on his teams. In fact, you almost knew if you got on his softball team or basketball team he was going to try to get to you. I could never understand why someone didn't do something about it. This went on for years; he was almost a legend around the place and seemed kind of invincible. Finally we got a principal who wouldn't put up with him anymore, and he was fired. My advice to you is this: Anything is possible. Get help. You never know how many others have had to put up with stuff from this character you're dealing with. Do everybody a favor.

It's Possible to Get Help

Dear Young & Alone:

I'm writing to you through Ted & Monica's column. I hope I can help you in this way.

I often have clients who have been sexually abused or who are being harassed into sexual liaisons. I know how difficult this whole situation is for you.

You can, however, do some things to help yourself. If you must continue to work in that situation, and only you can answer that question, then you must establish some defenses for yourself. You must be able to protect yourself.

I always tell my clients to pull a "circle of light" around themselves. Within this circle of light they will be protected. They will protect themselves. Once they are in the light they will know how to protect themselves. They will see. There are definite steps you can take to get to know yourself and your adversary better. There are definite methods you can employ to help you work out a good solution for you. I see from Ted & Monica's column that they are making excellent suggestions along those lines.

Once you are in the circle of light, you will know perfectly well how best to proceed for you. However you draw yourself into the light is fine. Some of my clients have learned to place themselves in the light through meditation. I do not suggest a very formal type of meditation, however. What I recommend is that you take yourself to a quiet spot for a few minutes each day and submerge yourself in the light.

The philosophers of the East tell us that all sin and evil is *maya*, or illusion. Goodness also is illusion. The world and everything in it is illusion. These philosophers practice meditation and learn to abandon *maya*, illusion. They enter the light; some of them even become "enlightened" persons. They learn to live in peace and harmony with the world. They are neither oppressors nor victims. They are happy people. By entering into a new relationship with the world they are able, through transformation of their own attitudes, to effect a transformation in those around them.

This may not seem like much of a solution to you. Carl Jung tells us, however, that unless human beings transform their hearts, there will be a great catastrophe on this earth. He did envision a terrible holocaust unless we transformed ourselves. We all have it within our power to transform ourselves and thereby to effect a change in others. You see, by your own ability to handle your unhealthy situation more positively, you may bring about a change in someone else.

Love. It all boils down to love. You must learn to love yourself and bring yourself into the light. And, lo and behold! perhaps this enemy of yours will be brought into the light by your own radiance. It has nothing to do with lust, but a lot to do with love.

This person who is harassing you is actually the victim. You possess much more power. You can effect lasting changes in your behavior and in the behavior of this harasser. Your harasser, however, has only threats to make, which can do little meannesses in limited ways for a definite period of time.

Be comforted and draw a circle of light around yourself.

Therapist

Dear Young & Alone:

Your letter to Ted & Monica reminded me of an incident that happened to me during World War II. I was stationed in Italy when I was approached by a second lieutenant in our unit. He made overtures to me. He wanted to have sex with me. We were a long way from home, and I was a pretty green kid. Nothing like that had ever happened to me before.

If the circumstances had been just a little different, I could have asked someone for advice. Or if I had just had a little more sophistication I would have handled it differently. As it was, I turned this guy down in no uncertain terms and told him where he could go. I did everything but slug him.

Within a few days I was shipped out of my unit. I was sent to North Africa and spent the rest of the war in a unit made up of prisoners from Joliet. I tell you, I will never forget the experience nor how hard the war years were for me after that.

I just wanted you to know that there are some of us out here who understand all about sexual harassment.

World War II Victim

Dear Ted & Monica:

I am a Marine. I joined up because I wanted to be a paramedic. I have put in for paramedical training every chance I got. Well, let me tell you, I am being shipped to Beirut next week and not as a paramedic. Why?

Because I turned down the offer an officer made to me

to become lovers. When I went to take the test to become a paramedic, they gave me a physical. One part of the physical was a urinalysis. They found traces in my urine of a substance that could only be there if I were a drug user. I have never even smoked pot since joining up two years ago, much less doing any other drug!

I am a very bitter man. I do what I'm told and say "Yes, sir" and "No, sir." But I hate them. I'm being shipped to one of the danger zones in the world, and all because I refused to have sex with some guy. He laughs at me now and even had the nerve to tell me that I was getting what I deserved.

Larry Leatherneck

Dear Ted & Monica:

I think your "friend" Young & Alone needs to see a shrink! Things like sexual harassment don't happen anymore. I never hear of such things. And since reading your columns lately, I've asked around among my friends. Nobody has ever had it happen to them or knows of anyone else who has been sexually harassed.

I guess things were getting a little dull in your column. Maybe you were losing readers to Dear Abby or Ann Landers. Haven't you carried this thing far enough?

Tired of Harassment Stories

Dear Ted & Monica:

I related to that letter from Young & Alone on a New Job. I had something like that happen to me once. I am a blind woman, and when I was very young I was in training to learn to operate vending machines. That is a good job for blind or partially sighted persons because it is easy to learn and, once you have learned, it is fairly routine work. You have to learn to fill the machines with snacks, empty the change from the machines, and keep them clean inside.

There are little things that you have to watch out for with the machines. The pack pusher can get stuck, and you have to go into the machine and get it unstuck so the packages of snacks come down like they're supposed to. The coffee, tea, hot chocolate, and "Cup-a-Soup" machines are more work because sometimes sugar or cream gets spilled on the hoses that lead from the canisters to the cup and you have to take the hoses off and clean them.

Anyway, I had this boss who was trying to train me, and whenever I had to get inside the machine to fill it or clean it, he would get in with me. The inside of a vending machine is not big enough for two people to stand without getting very close. That was the whole idea, I guess. He always got in the machine when I did and tried to get a good feel of me. I finally had enough and just said to him one day: "Hey, look! I can handle this myself, and if you don't leave me alone I'm going to report you to your boss!" That took care of it, and I never had any more trouble. Sometimes you just have to tell someone you mean business and act like you know your rights.

Virtuous Vendor

Dear Ted & Monica:

When I was in college, the head of the department (education) solicited sex from me and another woman in my class. We were both promised graduate assistantships if we would "be nice" to him. We were scared to do anything about it, because it seemed like it was just "our word against his." But we filed suit against him for sexual harassment. We won our case and a lot of money, and we both got our assistantships at other universities. The "professor" was fired.

Higher Education

Dear Ted & Monica:

I hope you realize that since women have risen to positions of power, they play the game just as well as men and have their victims of sexual harassment, too. They offer sex for rewards in the "company," too.

Shoe on the Other Foot

Dear Ted & Monica:

There is a teacher in our school who takes her special pets to her home a lot. She has fondled one or two of the boys and displayed herself to the girls. Once she changed clothes right in front of them.

None of the parents know about this yet. The boys are all anxious to have sex with her; the girls want to find out stuff about sex from her. Nobody tells on her. She is real nice to the kids, and everybody likes her. Except that she has some pets.

Eighth Grader

Dear Ted & Monica:

Sexual harassment is a crime! It is a misdemeanor in some states; in some states, however, it is a felony. You simply have to be aware of the statutes where you live. You can take someone to court for sexual harassment!

There was a case in our state recently where a surgeon was convicted of sexually harassing the nurse he worked with in the OR. She took him to court and he lost everything. Everything!

However, she had witnesses. One day he followed her into the lounge area (which he thought was empty) and struck her. There was someone in the toilet who heard

the whole thing. So she had him on assault charges, too.
Law Enforcer

Dear Ted & Monica:

I was sexually harassed on the job once. It got to be unbearable. I knew my rights, but I didn't know how to assert them. I knew I could take the man to court and sue, but I didn't have any witnesses to the harassment and I felt my case wouldn't hold up. It would have been his word against mine. I didn't want to go through all that ugliness. It looked like just too much of a hassle.

So I quit my job. It takes an awful lot of strength to deal with harassment of any kind, not just sexual. Sexual harassment is particularly demeaning, though. I just didn't have the strength to deal with it. It meant more to me to be able to work in peace. So I quit and found another job.

It is very hard for a victim of sexual harassment to have the courage to go through a court trial, or even to accuse someone to his/her boss. They often try to discredit you in court, make you look guilty or cheap or as if you had really seduced this person. I didn't want to subject myself to all that; I'd been through too much already.

So, for pcacc of mind, and just simply to get on with my life, I left that place and went to work somewhere else. I realize that just lets harassers think they can get away with it, but who wants to be a victim in court, too, and take all that the opposing lawyer dishes out?
Too Tired for Court

Dear Ted & Monica:

When I was in college another woman in our dorm had a very frightening experience. As a child she had had throat surgeries and, as a result, could talk only in a very low, soft voice. It was almost a whisper. To help with her tuition, she worked part time in the administration offices of the college.

Her supervisor, who was the dean of admissions, constantly harassed her. He told her he would rape her if he got the chance, and that he knew she wouldn't even be able to scream for help.

I wanted her to go with me to the president of the co"ege, but she refused. She was terribly frightened, mc.e so I think, of the consequences of reporting this ma." than of what he could do to her. I went to the president by myself. I had seen and heard him making passes at her, so I was a witness to the abuse. The dean of admissions got a two-week suspension without pay and was allowed to return to his job!

Witness

Dear Ted & Monica:

There is a man who works in another city for our company, a large nationwide insurance company. However, we learn all the major scuttlebutt of the company, especially if we work in sales as I do.

This man has had charges of sexual harassment brought against him to his supervisors. No punitive measures have been taken against him yet, but he has been put on notice that he is under close surveillance and if there is any reason to doubt that he has "cleaned up his act," he will be fired.

Insurance Agent

Dear Ted & Monica:

Once several years ago I became very interested in the peace movement. I decided to join a large peace group in this city that is made up of university professors, ministers from every denomination, priests, rabbis, business leaders, and so on. It was a very impressive gathering of high-minded people.

On one occasion we invited a national figure to speak to our group at a fund-raising dinner. I was seated at a table of eight, among whom were some religious leaders. In the middle of the meal the cleric seated next to me put his hand under the table and began stroking my leg.

I got up from the table, took my plate, and moved elsewhere. To the astonishment of everyone at the table, I explained my action by looking at the offending cleric and remarking that I expected to be treated like a lady and not subjected to unwanted sexual contact.

Not "Peace at Any Price"

Dear Ted & Monica:

Recently I was sitting on a park bench at about 11 o'clock at night with a friend of mine, another man. We were quietly talking. We were not drinking, doing dope, or doing anything other than sitting on a park bench, talking. Suddenly a policeman approached us and arrested us. We were doing nothing, I assure you, but talking.

He put us in his squad car and literally raced through city traffic as if we were top-priority criminals. He was doing almost 100 mph according to the speedometer. We were booked on vagrancy charges and held overnight at the county jail. Before we were let go (with the charges dismissed) the next morning, we were verbally abused by guards as being queer, fags, or queens. I did not even feel like an American citizen when I got out of that jail. If such things can happen to law-abiding citizens, what is the meaning of freedom?

If we had been doing anything at all, even carrying concealed weapons, that would have justified the arrest and the high-speed run to the jail, I would not be so bitter. We were not making an exhibition of ourselves; we were talking. That incident took away from me something that I doubt I will ever regain, my pride in being a member of a free society.

Not Guilty

Dear Ted & Monica:

I am a high school teacher who is tired of the verbal abuse and harassment I have to take from kids. I am constantly called "faggot" or "fag" by students in my classes or in the halls. When I complain about this to the principal, he says there is nothing he can do about it, that it is my problem.

The discipline in that school is so bad that I agree with him to a point. The kids don't do anything anybody tells them about anything. Why would they stop merely calling someone names when they engage in many other forms of abuse and get away with it?

The kids need to be taught a lesson, and I've considered getting legal representation. That seems too emotionally draining and possibly damaging to my career, however. Besides, I would be too embarrassed to have my girlfriend think I might really be gay. I don't know if I could live down the "image."

I can't afford to quit. All my education has been in this field. I don't understand why we don't have the right to work in a public school without being harassed and made fools of.

Harassed Teacher

Chapter IX

Finding Oneself—Ted & Monica's Column

Dear Readers:

We promised you another column about the victim of sexual harassment. We hope in this column to give you some tips on how to find out more about yourself. The more you know (even about yourself!) the better able you will be to stand up to aggression of any kind. As usual, we have our friends the experts to thank for all the help given us in this area of approaching self-knowledge.

We wish to begin with a self-survey. The purpose of the survey is to help you determine how you feel about yourself in certain situations and relationships. Once you make that determination, we hope you will be able to see where you need to practice more skills and gain in strength. We have never known anyone to achieve 100 percent on this skills inventory, and, indeed, it takes a high degree of maturity to score in the 81 to 100 percent range at all. Following the inventory is an interpretive analysis for your assistance.

Below is a list of statements with three options from which to choose in determining your attitudes and usual behavior patterns. At the end of the survey we will tell you how to score yourself.

Inventory of Personality Skills

Circle the answer (A, B, or C) that most nearly reflects your habitual attitude or behavioral pattern:

1. I feel comfortable talking on the phone to my friends when my parents are in the same room and can hear me.
   A. Always   B. Sometimes   C. Never

2. I hesitate to tell my parents things that happen at school, on dates, or in my life in general.
   A. Rarely   B. Sometimes   C. Always

3. I am embarrassed when my parents come to school for parents' nights or come to my place of employment.
   A. Rarely   B. Sometimes   C. Always

4. I wish my parents were like the parents of some of my friends.
   A. Rarely   B. Sometimes   C. Always

5. I wish my family were more like some that I've read about or seen in movies or on TV.
   A. Rarely   B. Sometimes   C. Always

6. I have a great time at family reunions.
   A. Always   B. Sometimes   C. Never

7. I think my parents interfere too much in my life.
   A. Rarely   B. Sometimes   C. Always

8. I can trust my parents to keep a secret.
   A. Always   B. Sometimes   C. Never

9. My parents laugh at me and tell jokes about me to others.
   A. Never   B. Sometimes   C. Often

10. I seem to do everything right at home.
    A. Usually   B. Sometimes   C. Rarely

11. I try out new ideas.
    A. Often   B. Sometimes   C. Rarely

12. I say what I believe no matter what anyone else thinks.
    A. Always B. Sometimes C. Rarely
13. I find new routes to go to school or to work.
    A. Often B. Sometimes C. Never
14. I try out new recipes for food.
    A. Often B. Sometimes C. Never
15. I fix my own car or bike if something breaks down.
    A. Usually B. Sometimes C. Never
16. I know how to get myself out of an emotional slump.
    A. Usually B. Sometimes C. Rarely
17. I practice something till I get it right.
    A. Usually B. Sometimes C. Rarely
18. I stick with difficult things.
    A. Usually B. Sometimes C. Rarely
19. I tell myself that my peace of mind is more important than hanging in with something or someone that is a source of pain to me.
    A. Usually B. Sometimes C. Rarely
20. I go places by myself if I really want to go and can't find anyone to go with me.
    A. Often B. Sometimes C. Rarely
21. I have things I like to do by myself, like reading or listening to music.
    A. Often B. Sometimes C. Rarely
22. I think I am an interesting person.
    A. Usually B. Sometimes C. Rarely
23. I tell jokes well.
    A. Usually B. Sometimes C. Rarely
24. I am the life of the party.
    A. Sometimes B. Usually C. Rarely
25. When I get into a funk I stay away from everybody.

A. Sometimes   B. Usually   C. Never
26. I lie to people.
   A. Often   B. Sometimes   C. Never
27. I have stolen things in the past.
   A. Never   B. Sometimes   C. Often
28. I try to cover up my mistakes.
   A. Rarely   B. Sometimes   C. Often
29. I laugh about my mistakes.
   A. Usually   B. Sometimes   C. Rarely
30. I think people think I am stupid.
   A. Rarely   B. Sometimes   C. Usually
31. I tell people about my achievements.
   A. Sometimes   B. Usually   C. Rarely
32. I brag.
   A. Rarely   B. Sometimes   C. Often
33. I am well coordinated.
   A. Yes   B. So-so   C. No
34. I work well with my hands.
   A. Yes   B. So-so   C. No
35. I think fast.
   A. Yes   B. So-so   C. No
36. My reaction time is good.
   A. Yes   B. So-so   C. No
37. I make fast replies.
   A. Yes   B. So-so   C. No
38. I say the right things.
   A. Yes   B. So-so   C. No
39. I can make people laugh.
   A. Yes   B. So-so   C. No
40. People get my message clearly.
   A. Yes   B. So-so   C. No
41. People take offense at what I say.
   A. Rarely   B. Sometimes   C. Often
42. I say stupid things.
   A. Rarely   B. Sometimes   C. Often

43. There are things I wish I hadn't said.
    A. Rarely   B. Sometimes   C. Often
44. I don't know why I say or do some things.
    A. Rarely   B. Sometimes   C. Often
45. I am attractive.
    A. Yes   B. So-so   C. No
46. I am sexually attractive.
    A. Yes   B. So-so   C. No
47. I think sex is (or will be) a good experience.
    A. Yes   B. Not sure   C. No
48. I think sex is best when you love your partner.
    A. Yes   B. Not sure   C. No
49. I think sex is there for the asking, and I don't mind who asks me.
    A. No   B. Sometimes   C. Yes
50. If I thought sex was the only way to get ahead, I'd use it.
    A. No   B. Maybe   C. Yes
51. I am afraid of doing the wrong thing.
    A. Rarely   B. Sometimes   C. Usually
52. I am afraid of teachers.
    A. Rarely   B. Sometimes   C. Usually
53. I think bosses are like teachers, always ready to criticize.
    A. Rarely   B. Sometimes   C. Usually
54. I think people in charge like to humiliate those under them.
    A. Rarely   B. Sometimes   C. Usually
55. What matters most is how much the person in authority likes me.
    A. No   B. Sometimes   C. Yes
56. Anybody would have sex with a boss, given the chance.
    A. No   B. Maybe   C. Yes
57. I can let myself be used as long as I am fully

aware of it.
A. No   B. Maybe   C. Yes

58. I control the situation even if I am being used.
A. No   B. Maybe   C. Yes

59. I can always get out when I want to even if I am being used.
A. No   B. Maybe   C. Yes

60. I think others would respect me if I had sex with my boss (teacher, professor, etc.)
A. No   B. Maybe   C. Yes

61. I think others would be jealous of my relationship with the boss (etc.).
A. No   B. Maybe   C. Yes

62. I would have power if I had a sexual relationship with my boss (etc.).
A. No   B. Maybe   C. Yes

63. I have difficulty relating to authority.
A. No   B. Sometimes   C. Yes

64. I have a lot of friends I can trust.
A. Yes   B. Some   C. No

65. My friends would stick by me through thick and thin.
A. Yes   B. Some   C. No

66. I have a good reputation.
A. Yes   B. Maybe   C. No

67. I talk about other people and like to see them fail.
A. No   B. Sometimes   C. Yes

68. When others are down, I must be up.
A. No   B. Maybe   C. Yes

69. For someone to win, someone else must lose.
A. No   B. Maybe   C. Yes

70. I am well liked.
A. Yes   B. Maybe   C. No

71. My teachers think I am creative.

A. Yes   B. Sometimes   C. No
72. I can think of better ways of doing things.
    A. Usually   B. Sometimes   C. Rarely
73. I can solve my own problems.
    A. Usually   B. Sometimes   C. Rarely
74. Other people come to me with their problems.
    A. Often   B. Sometimes   C. Rarely
75. I have a lot of problems.
    A. Usually   B. Sometimes   C. Rarely
76. I talk most of the time when I'm with others.
    A. Rarely   B. Sometimes   C. Usually
77. Other people like me because I listen a lot.
    A. Usually   B. Sometimes   C. Rarely
78. People come to me because I know all the answers.
    A. Rarely   B. Maybe   C. Rarely
79. I am afraid other people are going to get ahead of me.
    A. Rarely   B. Sometimes   C. Usually
80. I will do whatever I have to do to keep others from getting ahead of me.
    A. No   B. Maybe   C. Yes
81. Success is getting ahead of everybody else.
    A. No   B. Maybe   C. No
82. Success is doing my best.
    A. Yes   B. Maybe   C. No
83. Success is using people and things to my best advantage.
    A. No   B. Maybe   C. Yes
84. I am afraid I am going to be a failure.
    A. No   B. Maybe   C. Yes
85. I am a failure.
    A. No   B. Maybe   C. Yes
86. I am afraid of life.
    A. No   B. Maybe   C. Yes

87. Sex is what I do best.
    A. No   B. Maybe   C. Yes
88. I must be the top person at my job (or school, etc.) or I am a failure.
    A. No   B. Maybe   C. Yes
89. I will be liked only if I am the best.
    A. No   B. Maybe   C. Yes
90. I will have friends only if I can prove that I am a success.
    A. No   B. Maybe   C. Yes
91. When we have our class reunion I want to be on top.
    A. Yes   B. Maybe   C. No
92. I will do anything to get on top.
    A. No   B. Maybe   C. Yes
93. Sex and business make a good partnership.
    A. No   B. Maybe   C. Yes
94. It doesn't matter how I get ahead; in a few years I can put it all behind me.
    A. No   B. Maybe   C. Yes
95. It's winning that counts, not how you play the game.
    A. False   B. Perhaps   C. True
96. "Everybody does it," and that makes it OK for me.
    A. No   B. Maybe   C. Yes
97. Why shouldn't I give a little so I can get a lot in return?
    A. No   B. Maybe   C. Yes
98. If I am asked to have sex by my boss (teacher, etc.) it is just because I am so charming.
    A. No   B. Maybe   C. Yes
99. Anyone would be honored to be offered sex and rewards by a boss (teacher, etc.).
    A. No   B. Maybe   C. Yes

100. I would like to have power.
    A. Yes B. Maybe C. No

To find your score on this Inventory of Personality Skills:

1. Give yourself 3 points for every A answer.
2. Give yourself 1 point for every B answer.
3. Give yourself 2 points for every C answer.
4. Total the points for the A and B answers and from this sum subtract the C points.
5. Divide your answer by 3 and you have the percentage rating for your personality skills. The closer you are to 100 percent, the greater are your strengths in personality skills.

Ex. 60 A responses = 180 points
      20 B responses = 20 points
      20 C responses = 40 points

$$\begin{array}{cc} 180 & 200 \\ +\ 20 & -\ 40 \\ \hline 200 & 160 \end{array} \qquad \frac{160}{3} = 53.33\%$$

Interpretation of Scores

1%–20%—Very Low Personality Skills, characterized by:

    a. fear of others
    b. low self-esteem
    c. insecurity
    d. poor sexual identity
    e. inability to assert self
    f. inability to establish personal power
    g. habitual depression

21%–40%—Limited Personality Skills, characterized by:
   a. short periods of depression
   b. instability (outbursts of temper, moodiness)
   c. withdrawal from people and activities
   d. insecurity about sexuality
   e. fear of risk-taking
   f. inappropriate response to challenging situations (immaturity, bravado, retreat)
   g. misunderstanding of use of power (mean, petulant, critical, abusively demanding)

41%–60%—Weak but Developing Personality Skills, characterized by:
   a. ambivalence about self (long on dreams, short on methods of achievement)
   b. uncertainty about status in groups (family, etc.)
   c. sexually active but with no clearly defined sense of *self* or sense of *mutuality* with sexual partner
   d. lacking power (easily manipulated by others, frustrated leadership qualities)

61%–80%—Good Personality Skills, characterized by:
   a. good relationship with family
   b. good relationship with peers
   c. comfortable with authority figures
   d. good sexual identity
   e. benevolent in use of power (like to help others)

81%–100%—Strong Personality Skills, characterized by:
   a. acknowledged place of power in relationships
   b. good sexual identity
   c. positive self-image
   d. goal-oriented
   e. happy

Other characteristics could be added to each category, but these should be sufficient to give you an idea of the kinds of things in which you are strong or weak. The really important outcome of all this is for you to decide how you can improve your skills and gain in personal strength and power. Personal power is the keystone of your character building. Without personal power you risk being a vulnerable person. Without personal power you lay yourself open to all kinds of attack, unfair treatment, abuse, and even—sexual harassment.

In his book *Man for Himself*, Erich Fromm describes the person with a productive character orientation as being in touch with his/her own power. Such a person has the ability to produce himself/herself. The productive person, according to Fromm, uses the potentialities (power) within, whereas the unproductive person is impotent (unpowerful). When a person relates to the world with a real sense of power, that person is productive, in Fromm's view.

We will talk about achieving power, becoming productive persons, and reducing vulnerability in another column.

Ted & Monica

Chapter X

Power—Ted & Monica's Column

Dear Readers:

The person who is seen as having power is the one who has options, who can make choices, and who is responsible. Such a person is an active person. The power this person wields comes from within. Power is not invested in someone from the outside. England's Prince Hal possessed power before he was crowned Henry V. He did not change overnight from a rapscallion who cavorted with Falstaff into a strong and powerful leader. He could not have achieved such a transformation. Hal's real power came from within; when he chose to do so, he led England as well as he had formerly appeared to be led by Falstaff.

Falstaff, on the other hand, emerges as one with very few options even though he is engaged in many activities. He manages some schemes but he refuses to take responsibility for what he does (*Henry V, The Merry Wives of Windsor*). Part of the humor of the Falstaff character comes from this real impotence in the man, his lack of personal power from within, his inability to be responsible for his actions. Hence, Falstaff is a buffoon. He is, further, a perfect foil for Prince Hal, who has a real sense of inner power. He is Hal's victim, just as he is the victim of the Merry Wives of Windsor.

Ted

I suppose I would say that Falstaff is more acted upon than acting. That seems to make him a passive person, although passivity doesn't seem an accurate depiction of Falstaff.

Monica

I would say his passivity is what makes him a buffoon. It is that, more than anything else, which turns him into a victim. He allows other people to do things to him and to outwit him.

Except in the ultimate battle where he uses his wits to play dead and not get killed. He did in that instance possess the power to stay alive.

He disliked confrontation, and in that respect he is like many victims of sexual harassment. They feel that if they do and say nothing the problem will go away.

Perhaps Falstaff did not take himself seriously. Is it possible that victims of sexual harassment or other forms of abuse simply do not take themselves seriously?

Perhaps. Or they do not know how to exercise personal power. Sometimes they assume a persona that is not really "themselves" in order to appear strong, tough, powerful.

That, I suppose, makes them more of a challenge to the potential harasser? It creates a desire in the harasser to break down the defenses of this pseudo-powerful person?

Exactly. And that intimidates the impotent person even more. Then he/she will really shy away from the harassing person. In panic the potential victim backs off, and that sets him/her up for more harassment.

I notice you used the term *potential* victim. Would you say, then, that someone has the *power* to be a victim? You also referred to the victim as an *impotent* person. Would it be fair to say that a powerless person has the power to be victimized?

If you understand that the so-called powerless person

is simply one who hasn't realized his/her power, then you are correct. Each of us has real power; it is just a question of wanting to use it. When Falstaff chose to use his power, he saved his life. On the other hand, when he allowed others to act upon him, he was a fool.

Obviously, then, power must mean different things to different people.

Power can have negative connotations to many people. The very word power can cause some people to think:

1. Shark—someone out for blood;
2. Queen bee—someone who kills off the competition;
3. Power-hungry—someone greedy and evil.

On the other hand, power wielders can also be viewed as:

1. "The force"—all that is good, benevolent, caring, and nurturing dependent on good power;
2. Charismatic—possessing a gift, talent, given to few;
3. "The ring"—a network of people with connections;
4. "The insiders"—those with inside information;
5. Accessors—those who have access to the top;
6. "Know-it-alls'—the experts.

Power is style. It comes from within. There is power in

a Gershwin song ("The Man I Love"). There is a different kind of power in Sir Edward Elgar's "Pomp and Circumstance" marches. Power can be extravagant, baroque, stingy, mean, truthful, humorous, just, cruel.

Power can also be:
1. aggressive;
2. damaging;
3. stress-producing;
4. scary;
5. ruthless.

That is the kind of power that went out when democracies came in. That is the kind of power that often existed between kings and their subjects and between masters and their serfs. The rule of thumb was (and still is in places in the world where those systems exist): "If it's a choice of being loved or being feared—be feared!"

Or power can be:
1. nurturing;
2. caring;
3. compassionate;
4. creative;
5. diversified.

Power can be either harsh and uncompromising or compassionate and nurturing. It depends on "style."

In the movie "The Heavenly Kid," Bobby, the guardian angel/father, advises his teenage charge (his son) to "get some style." With style Lenny would have power over women, over machines, and over his competitors. The humor in the movie arises from Lenny's bumbling attempts to adopt a style that is not his own, a pseudo-power. Everything is eventually resolved when Lenny "finds himself." He finds his power; it was there all along in his own inimitable style.

The saying is that: "One who has never experienced love cannot give love." Style/power is something like that. It can be done, but if you have been repeatedly subjected to abuse, ridicule, and failure from infancy, you will have great difficulty in coming up with a style that connotes power. Are some people really set up from childhood to be life's victims?

Undoubtedly there are people (more than we'd like to acknowledge) who have been emotionally, physically, and intellectually victimized from babyhood. They have in some way threatened the domains and lives of the adults into whose care they were given. They are everywhere, on both sides of the tracks, in rich homes and poor ones.

It is much harder for persons from abusive backgrounds to develop a style that signifies power. It is much harder for them to develop a style that signifies a power that is productive in Erich Fromm's definition: A power *of*, which means a capacity *for*; not a power *over*, which means domination. Often abused persons become abusers themselves; they develop power, but it is the power over (to dominate) rather than the power of (capacity).

To avoid becoming (or remaining) an abused person, it is essential to develop the power of productiveness. It is absolutely vital, in order not to remain vulnerable and victimized, for these persons to move toward integration with the world so that they may exercise the power of love, humor, creativity, and generosity.

That is the goal for all; it is merely more difficult to achieve for those who have been deeply hurt by the psychological and physical beatings they have received from their elders during childhood. The goal for all is to be in tune with self and in harmony with the world. Then there is style. The way you do that is YOUR style. And that is power.

Once he had achieved his own style/power Lenny ("The Heavenly Kid") won the best girl, won the race, and did in the competition. He did it all with just a little help from his guardian angel/father.

We have spent a lot of time developing this theme of style/power. We happen to think it is very important in the whole question of sexual harassment.

Ted

Does that mean you're putting the whole responsibility for sexual harassment on the shoulders of the victim? It seems to me, Monica, that you're saying that if a person handles himself/herself properly the harassment won't occur?

Monica

What I'm saying is that the style/power of the victim will make a big difference in how the harassment is resolved. It is important to keep in mind that the harasser may be a dangerous person. The situation may need to be defused very carefully.

I think it is more important for the victim of sexual harassment to know definite steps, procedures that can be taken when harassment occurs.

That is true. There are specific things that can be done, but my point is that the first step is already in effect when the victim acts from a sense of innate style/power. The woman who wrote us about how she had moved her food from the table and publicly faced the harasser with what he had done took that first step. She approached the situation from a sense of her personal style/power.

That is true, but I think there was more she then could have done. I think she stopped too soon.

I agree with you there, Ted, and we must talk about that in a later column.

We can't emphasize how important it is, however, to develop your style/power. It is this aura you emit of productivity, of being a person who can produce yourself, as well as results, that will help you protect yourself in situations of harassment. This kind of style/power is like having money in the bank. Once it is there, and there is a lot of it, you can draw on it any time you need it. It may not keep you from being harassed, from being victimized, but it will make all the difference in the world in balancing your account.

Francis Bacon said: "The monuments of wit survive the monuments of power." In cases of real survival, however, one must often use one's wits in achieving a personal style/power. Like Falstaff.

Ted & Monica

Chapter XI

What to Do about Sexual Harassment—Ted & Monica's Column

Dear Readers:

It is important, in developing your personal style/ personal power, to be aware that you have the law behind you in cases of sexual harassment. You are not alone. The law, the Constitution, the lower courts, and the Supreme Court are on your side.

On October 23, November 1, and November 13, 1979, the House of Representatives Subcommittee on Investigations of the Committee on Post Office and Civil Service of the Ninety-Sixth Congress of the United States held hearings on sexual harassment in the federal government. The hearings brought forth information from surveys conducted by private groups (such as *Red Book* magazine) as well as by government employees.

An unofficial survey by the Department of Housing and Urban Development found that 160 females had reported being sexually harassed. New Responses, a small, nonprofit organization of women's policy consultants that surveyed government employees, found that 40 percent of the nearly 200 respondents to their survey had been sexually harassed. Of the more than 9,000 women who answered the *Red Book* questionnaire, 9 out of 10 had been sexually harassed on the job. The testimony of one witness before the Subcommittee (Donna Lenhoff, staff attorney, Women's Legal Defense

Fund) brought out that probably 70 percent of women in the work force have experienced sexual harassment. Barbara Somson of the International Union of Electrical and Machine Workers (IUE) reported that between 50 and 90 percent of working women have experienced sexual harassment on the job.

Ms. Lenhoff's testimony to the Subcommittee contained this definition of sexual harassment:

> Sexual harassment is any repeated or unwarranted verbal or physical sexual advances, sexually explicit derogatory statements, or sexually discriminatory remarks made by someone in the workplace which is offensive or objectionable to the recipient or which causes the recipient discomfort or humiliation or which interferes with the recipient's job performance.[1]

Sexual harassment may include:

1. any undesired and unsolicited sexual attention on the job;
2. stares;
3. leers;
4. sexual innuendoes;
5. propositions through touching, kissing, or physical assault;
6. asking or requiring sexual favors in return for employment opportunities;
7. patting, pinching, poking;
8. suggestions accompanied by threats.

Thus, the researchers found, some forms of sexual harassment are overt whereas others are more subtle and hidden. Some forms of sexual harassment are physical; others are purely verbal or in the nature of threats.

Ms. Largen, a member of New Responses, categorized the problem in two ways: "inducement" and "harassing behavior." She defined each of these behaviors in this way.

> Inducement, as a form of sexual harassment, describes a situation where sexual compliance is proposed or exchanged for a job or job opportunities. The proposition may or may not be accompanied by a job threat or other forms of coercion.
>
> Harassing behavior, on the other hand, describes situations where no job opportunity offers are made, but where the victims are subjected to behaviors ranging from nonphysical acts such as leers and innuendoes to pinching, patting, and other forms of direct physical contact. Although suggestions or propositions may be made along with this behavior, they may or may not be accompanied by job threats or other pressures.[2]

Sexual harassment does not always lead to criminal acts, but people who have been harassed sometimes are raped or murdered. Harassment itself is an insidious act of violence. It is not inconceivable that other acts of violence, criminal acts of serious violence, could be a consequence of sexual harassment. Whether the harassment is by inducement, with the offer of rewards for sexual favors, or is already violent in that the victim is subjected to unwanted physical or verbal attention, the outcome may be serious harm to the victim. In sexual harassment the victim is *acted upon*, subjugated to the will and demands of others.

We have said there could be loss of life or rape. What other harmful things could happen to the victim?

Other Harmful Effects of Sexual Harassment

1. Loss of job
2. Loss of job without compensation
3. Stress for self and family
   a. Victim's credibility is questioned:
      i. Does victim dress, talk, and act appropriately?
      ii. Is victim actually to blame for causing harassing behavior?
      iii. Victim is often unable to obtain witnesses, as much harassment occurs in private.
   b. Victim's family is often called upon to be witnesses
   c. Possible retaliation against the victim by management:
      i. Demotion
      ii. Increase of workload with no corresponding monetary compensation
      iii. Attempt to make workplace so miserable that victim will quit:
         a. Victim's office changed to unpleasant area (dark, dingy, small, airless)
         b. Victim given shift not preferred
         c. Victim continually criticized for "unsatisfactory" work
      iv. Poor evaluation
      v. Rejection of victim's bid for promotion
      vi. "Unsatisfactory" recommendation for résumé
4. Long waiting period between filing of complaint and any resolution of the problem, during which time:

a. Victim may be intimidated
b. Victim is discouraged from proceeding with complaint
c. Victim's job insecurity is increased
d. Victim's job performance is negatively affected
e. Victim often becomes prey to more harassment (sometimes from other sources)
f. Victim may be fired (ostensibly for something else)
g. Victim may be transferred
h. Victim's job may be "abolished."

The reports to the Subcommittee contained suggestions for dealing with sexual harassment. There are actions that companies (in this case the federal government is the employer in question) can take to reduce sexual harassment in the workplace:

Methods for Reducing Sexual Harassment in the Workplace

1. Employer-sponsored training programs to instruct all employees about sexual harassment in the workplace, including:
   a. Definition of sexual harassment
   b. Definite guidelines relating to sexual harassment
   c. Penalties for sexual harassment
   d. Procedures for reporting sexual harassment:
      i. in-house chain of command
      ii. Personnel department
   e. Statutes of that state regarding sexual harassment, its interpretation and punishment.
2. Unemployment compensation for victims who quit jobs because of sexual harassment
3. Less red tape for reporting sexual harassment

4. Shorter time between initial reporting of harassment and action taken on charges
5. Clear statement of in-house investigative policy toward charges of harassment
6. Clear statement of in-house support for victim's rights during investigation
7. Clear statement of action to be taken at conclusion of in-house investigation:
   a. What will be done to harasser?
   b. What, if any, compensation will be made to victim?
8. Clear statement of extent of cooperation with civil authorities in the event the victim charges the harasser in a civil suit.
9. Information about Title VII of the Civil Rights Act of 1964.

It is the Civil Rights Act of 1964 that guarantees persons' rights against sexual harassment in the workplace because it stipulates that persons shall not be discriminated against because of sex. In the section of the act relating to "Unlawful Employment Practices," the law states:

It shall be an unlawful employment practice for an employer-

(1) To fail or refuse to hire or to discharge any individual, or otherwise to discriminate against any individual with respect to his compensation, terms, conditions, or privileges of employment, because of such individual's race, color, religion, sex, or national origin.

(2) To limit, segregate, or classify his employees or applicants for employment in any way which would deprive or tend to deprive any individual of

employment opportunities or otherwise adversely affect his status as an employee, because of such individual's race, color, religion, sex, or national origin.[3]

These provisions of the Civil Rights Act of 1964 extend to employment agencies, training programs, labor unions, and seniority and merit systems. The provision of the Act is clear about discrimination for compensation and/or merit.

Notwithstanding any other provision of this subchapter, it shall not be an unlawful employment practice for an employer to apply different standards of compensation, or different terms, conditions, or privileges of employment pursuant to a bona fide seniority or merit system, or a system which measures earnings by quantity or quality of production or to employees who work in different locations, provided that such differences are not the result of an intention to discriminate because of race, color, religion, sex, or national origin, nor shall it be an unlawful employment practice for an employer to give and to act upon the results of any professionally developed ability test provided that such test, its administration or action upon the results is not designed, intended or used to discriminate because of race, color, religion, sex, or national origin. It shall not be an unlawful employment practice under this subchapter for any employer to differentiate upon the basis of sex in determining the amount of wages or compensation to be paid to employees of such an employer if such differentiation is authorized by the provision of Section 206 (D of Title IX).[4]

The Merit Systems Protection Board was given specific responsiblities under the Reform Act as it applies to Title VII of the Civil Rights Act of 1964. Testimony to the Subcommittee in 1979 included this statement about the Merit Board:

"As you know, sex discrimination in violation of Title VII of the Civil Rights Act of 1964, as amended, is specifically designated as a prohibited personnel practice under the Reform Act. It has been held that some forms of sexual harassment are considered sex discrimination within the meaning of Title VII.

"Additionally, the Reform Act forbids, as prohibited personnel practices, other types of behavior which could occur as a result of sexual harassment, including:

"Considering any recommendation unless that recommendation is based on the merits of an individual's performance;

"Granting any preference not otherwise available by law for the purpose of improving or injuring the prospects of any particular person for employment;

"Taking or failing to take a personnel action in reprisal for revealing a violation of law, rule, or regulations, including sexual harassment; and

"Discriminating on the basis of conduct which does not adversely affect performance.

"The Reform Act provides the Special Counsel of the Board [Merit Systems Protection Board] with a wide range of investigatory and prosecutorial tools to uncover and prosecute those who engage in prohibited personnel practices, including sexual harassment."[5]

In a judgment handed down on June 19, 1986 (*Vinson* vs. *Meritor Savings Bank*) the Supreme Court of the United States ruled unanimously that sexual harassment of an employee by a supervisor is a violation of Title VII of the Civil Rights Act of 1964. It is a violation of this federal law against sex discrimination in the workplace.

That Supreme Court decision differed somewhat from a Ninth Circuit case, *Miller* vs. *Bank of America*, 1979, in that the Court in the Miller case held that an employer was responsible for an employee's harassing behavior. Even though a company had a clear-cut policy prohibiting supervisors from sexually harassing employees, that did not relieve the company of responsibility in the event such harassment did occur.

The majority of the Justices in the *Vinson* vs. *Meritor* opinion did not hold the view that companies are always responsible for the sexually harassing behavior of their employees.

> "Justice Rehnquist's opinion said that an employer's liability depends on the circumstances. He added that an employer's lack of knowledge of harassment by a supervisor 'does not necessarily insulate that employer from liability,' but he declined 'to issue a definitive rule on employer liability.'"[6]

Referring to this decision, an article in *The Wall Street Journal* of June 24,1986, said:

> "In a ruling last week, the Supreme Court significantly expanded the circumstances in which sexual harassment may be a violation of federal civil-rights law. The Court said that workers may sue their employers for sex discrimination on the grounds that

sexual harassment by supervisors created a hostile job environment, even if loss of job or promotion wasn't involved. But the court rejected a lower-court ruling that a company is always liable for sexual harassment of workers by supervisors, even if company management wasn't aware of the problem. At the same time, however, the Court ruled that a company isn't necessarily insulated from liability just because management wasn't notified of the problem."[7]

What this Supreme Court decision did accomplish, however, was to make a statement about sexual harassment in the workplace. It established definitively that sexual harassment is a violation of Title VII of the Civil Rights Act of 1964, an Act that prohibits racial and sexual discrimination.

The United States Chamber of Commerce had argued that, because the alleged sexual harassment of a female subordinate by her male supervisor had not resulted in any loss of money or job benefits, there was no violation of Title VII in that no sex discrimination took place.

"Justice Rehnquist, on the other hand, ruled that 'when a supervisor sexually harasses a subordinate because of the subordinate's sex, that supervisor discriminates on the basis of sex'.

"He said, 'Courts have uniformly held, and we agree, that a plaintiff may establish a violation of Title VII by proving that discrimination based on sex has created a hostile or abusive work environment.'

"Justice Thurgood Marshall, in a separate opinion joined by Justices William J. Brennan Jr., Harry A. Blackmun, and John Paul Stevens, said, 'I fully agree that workplace sexual harassment is illegal,' but he said that the Court had not gone far enough.

"He said employers should be held responsible whenever supervisors sexually harassed their subordinates, 'regardless of knowledge or any other mitigating factor,' following the Equal Employment Opportunity Commission guidelines adopted several years ago."[8]

Justice Rehnquist also said that a lower court had erred in the case of *Vinson* vs. *Meritor* by barring testimony about the sexual fantasies that Ms. Vinson talked about at work as well as about her provocative manner of dress. The case was sent back for further proceedings.

Thus, the *Vinson* vs. *Meritor* case is a bag of mixed blessings for victims of sexual harassment. There is a clear victory for those who have long argued that sexual harassment is a violation of Title VII of the Civil Rights Act, but certain aspects of the decision are not, in the opinion of some, quite strong enough.

What the Supreme Court Decision Does:

It makes a definitive statement that sexual harassment is a violation of a person's civil rights by stating that sexual harassment is in violation of Title VII of the Civil Rights Act of 1964.

What the Supreme Court Decision Does Not Do:

1. It does not hold that an employer is always responsible for the sexually harassing behavior of a supervisor toward a subordinate.
2. It does not consider the victim's dress, manner of speaking, and behavior as inadmissible evidence in a court case on sexual harassment. The attentions

to the victim may not have been "unwanted," and
the evidence for this would be in the victim's manner
of speech and dress.

The victim does, however, have the power of the law
behind him/her now. Title VII of the Civil Rights Act of
1964 does definitely protect one's right against sexual
harassment on the job because it is a form of sexual
discrimination. It is important to note, however, that the
Vinson vs. *Meritor* case was referred back to the lower
courts.

The interpretation of sexual harassment varies from
state to state, as does the punishment. States may have
narrow or broad definitions of sexual harassment. One
state may specify: "If you do thus and thus, you are
guilty of sexual harassment." Specific actions are spelled
out, and only within the limits of the definition can
behavior be termed sexually harassing. Another state
may be more liberal and thus have a broader interpretation of what constitutes sexual harassment: "These
actions, words and/or behaviors constitute sexual harassment, and violations of any or all of them are punishable
acts."

States also vary widely in sentencing for sexual harassment. In some states it is a misdemeanor; in others, a
felony.

Thus, although there is comfort in knowing that it is
the law of the land that sexual harassment is a criminal
act, in reality the protection afforded by the law may be
somewhat misleading. Much depends on the statutes on
sexual harassment in each state. Much depends on the
willingness of the employer to enforce practices that
absolutely discourage sexual harassment. Much still depends on the personal style/power of the person being
victimized.

We will have one more column on the topic of sexual harassment, Readers, and we hope to round out our discussion there. Thank you for your very helpful letters, both to us and to Young & Alone on a New Job.

Ted & Monica

Chapter XII

Problems in Coping with Sexual Harassment—Ted & Monica's Column

Dear Readers:

We come to our final column on sexual harassment, and today we wish to focus on the specifics of coping with it. Let us say at the outset that the whole matter of dealing with sexual harassment is a developing field. Neither the law nor the methodology for coping with it is fully developed yet. Some very knotty problems remain to be settled.

Ted

It seems that the law, as determined by *Vinson* vs. *Meritor Savings Bank*, refers only to supervisors who sexually harass subordinates.

Monica

That is definitely an area needing clarification, because sexual harassment can occur at any level. If we're talking just about "inducement," then the harassment must be by a superior. The very nature of inducement indicates that a reward is offered for an action or behavior.

Sexual harassment, however, is not always in the form of inducement. We know that it is often a case of harassment, pure and simple, with no offer of reward but the sexual act itself. This kind of harassing behavior can occur between equals or between persons holding lateral positions in a company.

Not only that, Ted, but sexual harassment can occur outside the actual place of employment. It can occur wherever people meet other people. It can come from taxi drivers, from restaurant workers, ushers in a theater, salespersons, insurance agents, clerks in a store, or from police officers.

The Civil Rights Act of 1964 protects people from discriminatory acts in the workplace. How, then, are people going to be protected who are in the places you mentioned, or who are students in high school or college?

Actually, students are in their "place of work." The school is the workplace for them, and heads of colleges or school systems have an obligation to see that students are not sexually harassed, at least by staff. In 1977 a class action suit was brought against Yale University for failure to investigate a charge of sexual harassment. The University was held responsible for this inaction and thus for seeming to condone the sexual harassment.

Well, but what of the woman who is chased around the coffee table in her own home by an insurance agent? What recourse to the law has she?

It can actually be held that the home, in that instance, is the woman's workplace. After all, she is involved in a legal business transaction at that time. The same argument ought to hold for persons harassed in restaurants, taxicabs, stores, beauty shops, and so on.

The victim in these cases does not share a mutual employer with the harasser. The victim may inform the employer of the harassing individual, but after that has recourse only to the law by virtue of a civil suit.

That is also true for self-employed men and women who are harassed by persons with whom they deal in business. They may actually be sexually harassed by clients. This type of harassment is not of the inducement kind; it is harassment only for the sake of obtaining sexual favors.

Well, Monica, it would, in fact, be inducement if the client threatened to withhold business on the basis of sexual favors, just as it would be inducement if a homeowner, say, agreed to purchase a product from a salesperson only if sex were part of the deal.

But, Ted, what about the case of the homeowner offering sexual favors to the salesperson without

> any inducement but the
> sexual act itself?

You mean, like the old
movies where the house-
wife would "get it on" with
the milkman?

> Exactly.

As you can see, Readers, many problem areas remain
as to what constitutes a workplace. We haven't even
ventured into the problem of sexual harassment as it
occurs in singles' bars, health clubs, resorts, or amusement parks. You can see all the difficulties in presenting
cases of this nature in courtrooms.

Around 1900 there was a cartoon featuring a young
woman called "Sallie Snooks." Sallie worked in an office
as a "type-writer," which is what a typist was then
called. The men in the office brought her gifts, crowded
around her desk to talk to her, and stopped their own
work to be attentive to Sallie. Sallie was fired by the boss
for "demoralizing" the other office workers.

By 1907 "Tillie the Toiler" had joined the force of
"type-writers" in comic-strip lore. In one episode Tillie's
friend Bubbles receives an expensive watch as a Christmas present from her boss, and Tillie points out to her
own boss how well Bubbles is treated. After a bit of
pouting and coy begging, Tillie then gets money from
the boss to go out and buy her own Christmas present.

Then "Flyin' Jenny" and "Myra North—Nurse" became comic-strip heroines around the time of World
War II. "Brenda Starr, Girl Reporter," was also popular
at the time. Brenda did do some reporting, but most of
her time was spent searching for her mysterious lover,
the man with the patch over one eye. Today, in "Apartment 3-G," the three women heroines work at different

jobs and are professionals. They are still, however, women who work for others and are not totally independent. Magee, one of these modern women, allowed herself to be romantically seduced (i.e., sexually harassed) into "losing" a contract for her own boss.

Women are now taken more seriously in the workplace. No longer are they merely the bread-makers. Many of them are breadwinners, perhaps the only breadwinner in the home. If this is the case, they are even more vulnerable. They desperately need their job to provide for themselves and, possibly, a family. They cannot afford to lose their job, lose pay, lose promotions.

Sexual harassment has been considered a women's issue. The 1979 Subcommittee hearings addressed it as a "women's issue," a gender-based problem. The women's groups have been largely responsible for bringing it into the foreground. Women in the workplace, the argument goes, have been demeaned, demoralized, and dehumanized by sexual harassment. With more and more women coming into the workplace every day, the potential for increased sexual harassment is obvious.

Sexual harassment, however, is not just a women's issue from the viewpoint of "women as victims of men." Nor is it a solely heterosexual activity. Lesbians engage in sexual harassment of other women. Gay men harass other men (gay or not) for sexual attentions. Finally, with more and more women achieving management positions, the inducements offered for sexual favors do not always come from male supervisors. Many lower and middle management jobs are now held by women, and they are in the same position as men to offer inducements for sexual favors.

What Freud did for humankind was to reveal that we all share the same propensities for evil. The "garbage" that he realized was hidden in the depths of the human psyche was not restricted by race, color, religion, sex, or national origin. All humans are capable of vile acts, thoughts, behaviors, and attitudes. Women, as well as men, are capable of sexually harassing behavior. Female chauvinism is just as oppressive as is male chauvinism.

Sexual harassment is a vile act based on lust and the desire to exercise power over someone else. It is a violent act that can lead to acts of more terrible violence. It is not restricted to men, to women, to heterosexuals, or to homosexuals. More acts of sexual harassment have been reported by women harassed by men, but that may not be unusual given the views of society on homosexuality.

What about the case of the two men talking quietly on a park bench who were arrested and detained overnight with no charges filed against them? Isn't that clearly an act of sexual harassment? Weren't they picked up because they *seemed* to be gays? And what of their stay in jail? Don't they have a right against sexual harassment from guards at the jail?

It may be far more stressful for someone to come forward and acknowledge that he/she has been the victim of homosexual harassment. The "guilt by association" hypothesis may be too much for a victim to handle. If women who are harassed by men suffer stress in protecting their image as "having done nothing to instigate the harassment," how much more stress must be endured by someone reporting homosexual harassment.

And then there is the problem of defining where sexual harassment ends and courtship begins. When men and women work together, there are bound to be legitimate romances. Should these be banned altogether? Should people be prohibited from marrying a co-worker? If you marry a co-worker must one of you leave the workplace and get another job? Can there be no spontaneity, no joy, in the workplace over sexual jokes, harmless teasing? *Is* there any harmless teasing when it comes to sex? Do we want our workplaces so homogenized, sterilized, and rid of sex-identifying dress and behavior that it takes totalitarian-state methods to enforce this "safe" environment? Big Brother/Big Sister is always watching to see that you don't slip and make any sexual inuendoes? How should we adapt to such a workplace?

A page one article in *The Wall Street Journal*, June 24, 1986, says:

> Sexual harassment is becoming an increasingly important management issue. The continuing surge of women into the work force—many of them single parents who are particularly vulnerable because of their financial situation—raises the potential for sexual harassment. And women are fighting back.
>
> Labor unions are educating their members about their rights and pressing management to take steps to prevent sexual harassment. Employer groups worry that companies will be required to police workplace romances to make sure they are voluntary.[1]

Ted   *Monica*

Men in business have always seemed to know how to dress. I mean, you just don't see male lawyers going into court dressed for the beach, Monica.

Women know how to dress professionally, too, Ted.

However, it is difficult for women to disguise the fact that they have mammary glands, and that feature of their bodies seems to get men really "bent out of shape." I don't see women dressed for the beach in law offices or elsewhere, for that matter, but I don't think that we need to ask women to have breast-reduction surgery because some men get overstimulated at the sight of ample breasts.

Perhaps we ought to have employers enforce dress codes.

How many schools or colleges have ever been able to enforce dress codes? And do you really think that putting people in sackcloth would reduce the occasions of sexual harassment? Come on, Ted, you know better than that.

Indeed I do, and I just played devil's advocate for you in this one, Monica. As you know, though, these are the kinds of things that trial lawyers still try to make out as issues, as relevant testimony in sexual harassment cases.

Even the Supreme Court ruling in *Vinson* vs. *Meritor* allows that a company may present testimony to the effect that a supervisor's attentions were not "unwanted," that the victim dressed and spoke in such a way that it seemed as if the sexual "attentions" of the supervisor were *desired* by the victim.

Let me continue to be devil's advocate for a bit, Monica. Suppose a supervisor (or other person) is falsely charged with sexual harassment? How is the company ever to know the truth and to protect its innocent employee? After all, we have acknowledged the usually secret nature of sexual harassment. It is conceivable, to me, anyway, that an innocent person could be ruined for life in a trial or company action resulting from false testimony about sexual harassment.

That is precisely the reason, Ted, why management has always been so protective of "its own." There has always been fear on the part of companies that innocent parties would be maligned. Of course, the supervisors in question have always assured management that that was the case. The "good ole boy" network has worked very well in that regard. Men have protected each other in the face of charges of harassment from female employees. Management, which has traditionally been male-dominated, has been part of the "good ole boy" network for a long, long time.

So, you see, Readers, how very difficult this subject of sexual harassment is. The law is there to protect you, but you had better be fully aware of all the difficulties before you use the law to back you up. You had better know the statute on sexual harassment in your state, what is the interpretation and what are the punishments.

You had better know exactly where your company stands on the issue before you take the job. You ask about salary, fringe benefits, health insurance, and vacation time. Ask also about the standards the company uses in complying with Title VII of the Civil Rights Act of 1964 as it applies to sexual harassment. Does it have training programs? What is the procedure for reporting violations if and when sexual harassment happens? What does management do about violations? This can present another knotty problem.

Ted	*Monica*
What if, in the chain of command you have been given to use in reporting sexual harassment, the supervisor to whom you should report is, in fact, the one who is harassing you?	
	What do you do? Do you bypass company policy altogether and get a lawyer? Or do you break the chain of command and go to the supervisor's supervisor, the manager's manager?
Or do you go to the personnel manager right off the bat?	

We still insist that one of the most important things for you to do is to establish your own personal style/power. The law may be behind you, but your own power and style may be your "ace in the hole." Particularly in dealing with all the stress related to sexual harassment, its reporting and its resolution, your inner strength, the way you deal with the issue, will be a deciding factor. The stronger you are, the more choices you will have.

Power/style may even be a factor in preventing you from becoming a victim of sexual harassment. The more strong-minded you become, and the more able you are to deal with your own sexuality, the better able you will be to deal with sexual harassment. Strong people seem to "have it all together." They are the ones others do not "mess with." And if harassment does occur, they are better able to come out and say: "I don't like what you're doing and saying. I want it to stop."

That is not inevitably true, though. You must remember that there are some "crazies" out there, some people who happen to find you in the "wrong place at the wrong time" and go after you. Even Lenny in "The Heavenly Kid" had a guardian angel, after all. It is important to have friends, family, loved ones, and professional counselors available to help you.

The women's movement has brought "networking" into prominence as a means for women to help each other in the work world. It is often referred to as the "mentor system" or the "sisterhood." Women realize that *together they are three times as strong*. Through networking they have an opportunity to talk to each other and to learn from each other. They have come to realize that they are not just "poor imitations of men." They respect each other and are trying to make the workplace a better place for all. There are professional groups for women, as well as specifically for gays and lesbians.

At the national level there are these resources for women:

National Organization of Women (NOW)
1401 New York Avenue NW
Washington, DC 20005

Women's Legal Defense Fund (national legal assistance group)
2000 P Street NW
Washington, DC 20036

More specifically for gays and lesbians there are:

LAMBDA (Legal Defense and Education Foundation)
132 West 43rd Street
New York, NY 10036

National Gay and Lesbian Task Force
80 Fifth Avenue
New York, NY 10011

Fund for Human Dignity
80 Fifth Avenue
New York, NY 10011

Human Rights Campaign Fund
Box 1396
Washington, DC 20013

Gay Rights National Lobby
P.O. Box 1892
Washington, DC 20013

A National Crisis Hot Line exists (the number for which can be obtained from local gay and lesbian groups), which is involved in documentation of incidents of sexual discrimination and sexual harassment.

The American Civil Liberties Union is a resource for all.

At the local level, Spouse Abuse Centers and Rape Relief Centers exist in most large cities. The Commission on Human Rights has local offices in large cities, as does the Equal Employment Opportunities Commission (EEOC). Legal Aid Societies can be a source of information, counsel, and help. There are professional organizations or unions for most jobs.

It is important to remember that, in spite of the law, in spite of Title VII of the Civil Rights Act of 1964, in spite of personal style/power, and in spite of support groups, some sexually harassed victims become victims of far more serious crimes. They become victims of rape or murder or both.

The Wall Street Journal article previously quoted says:

> Workplace atmosphere appears often to set the stage for violent sexual harassment. For example, the Equal Employment Opportunity Commission, in a lawsuit filed last November [1985] against ABC Rentals Inc. of Arlington, Texas, charged that supervisors' conduct at the company created a "sexually poisoned work environment." The EEOC suit, filed in a federal district court in Dallas, sought a temporary restraining order and preliminary injunction barring ABC from, among other things, sexually harassing its employees.
>
> In an affidavit for the EEOC, JoDel Bell Chapman said that in October 1983, three months after she started work at an ABC Rentals store in Fort Worth, Texas, her boss, Tony Bedford, during an evaluation pinned her against a workbench and demanded sex in return for a raise. When she refused, according to the affidavit, he raped her and threatened to fire her if she reported what had happened. After that, Mrs. Chapman's affidavit said, she got a small raise but then was raped twice more in the next year.[2]

And don't ever forget, Readers, that some persons who have resisted sexual harassment have been murdered. We recently heard of another case in a community near here. A young girl was murdered while she tended a store alone during lunch hour. The police caught and arrested the man, who was later convicted of murdering her because—she had refused to date him.

Ted & Monica

Chapter XIII

Diary Entry by Young & Alone

Dear Diary:
   I certainly have learned a lot from my communications with Ted & Monica, from their columns on sexual harassment, and from all the readers who have written both to them and to me in person. Let's see if I can put it all together so that it makes sense. Let's see, Dear Diary, if I've learned enough so that I can begin to put together the pieces of my life, get on with my job, and put my own experience of sexual harassment behind me.

What is sexual harassment?

Sexual harassment is any unwanted verbal or physical attention given with the intention of gaining sexual favors. It may be in the form of inducement, when someone is offered a reward or threatened in some way in return for sexual favors. It may be in the form of harassment that requires only sexual favors.
   Inducement occurs when a supervisor offers something or threatens to withhold something unless sex is given. The other form of harassment occurs between peers or when no reward or threat is part of the package.
   Sexual harassment is a violent crime. It is an act of violence by someone who desires to gain control or power over another human being and does so by satisfying his/her lustful urges. Because it is violent in its very

nature, it is not surprising when it ends in rape or even murder.

Sexual harassment can be overt or covert. The innuendoes my be very subtle, and the occasions of such innuendoes may be very secret. On the other hand, there may be all kinds of overt gestures, words, suggestions, actions, and behaviors.

To whom does sexual harassment happen?

1. Women have been the most victimized. This is especially difficult if they are:
   a. the source of the family income;
   b. their own sole support.
2. Men are more frequently the objects of sexual harassment as more and more women get middle management jobs.
3. ANYONE can be the victim of sexual harassment. It can be harassment of a heterosexual or homosexual nature.

Where does sexual harassment occur?

1. The workplace is the usual site, but sexual harassment also occurs wherever people are together:
   a. buses, taxis, planes, etc.
   b. health clubs, tennis courts, playing fields, pools, locker rooms, etc.
   c. crime-related harassment: jails, courts, police stations.
   d. meeting places: churches, clubs, civic associations, volunteer organizations, professional organizations.
   e. public places: restrooms, restaurants, stores, shopping malls, parks, libraries.

f. places of amusement: theaters, amusement parks, concerts, etc.
2. Sexual harassment can also occur at places of learning: schools, colleges and universities, and tutoring centers.
3. Sexual harassment can occur in the military.

Sexual harassment is a violation of Title VII of the Civil Rights Act of 1964. This is a federal law, binding everyone in the land. The individual states have laws about sexual harassment, but both the interpretation and the punishment vary from state to state. It may be a felony or a misdemeanor; it may be interpreted broadly or narrowly.

What should I do to prevent sexual harassment on the job?

1. When I apply for a job, I should ask certain things of my potential employer:
   a. Do you have a training-program about sexual harassment?
   b. What are your company policies about sexual harassment? I especially want to know what is the procedure for reporting sexually harassing behavior; do I go to the personnel director, to the supervisor, or (in case the supervisor is the one doing the harassing) to that supervisor's supervisor?
   c. What steps do you take if someone reports sexual harassment in your company?
   d. Do you have unemployment compensation for victims of sexual harassment who quit because of it?
   e. Do all your employees know that sexual harass-

ment is a violation of Title VII of the Civil Rights Act of 1964, and that there are also state laws pertaining to it? Do they know that sexual harassment is a crime?

2. When I take a job I need to establish my personal career goals and a time-line for the realization of those goals. I need to perfect my job skills so that I can reasonably expect to achieve my goals without being pressured into exchanging sexual favors for a shortcut to an unearned job reward. If I am to make it to the top in my career, I am going to receive my promotions because of my job performance and not because I gave sex to someone.

3. I need to acquaint myself with the professional organizations and the unions available to me through my job. These groups could offer me an important way of networking. I can meet people who will offer me help, advice, and counsel in my professional life. These groups may have valuable things to teach me about problems that I face, even sexual harassment. Who knows? I may find mentors who will really help me to advance in legitimate ways in my career.

4. I need to be aware of all the professional groups on the national, state, or local level that can offer advice or even assistance in case of sexual harassment. I need to know how much backing I will get from them in case I ever need it.

5. I need to surround myself with loving people. I need to have a net around me of caring, nurturing, loving family and friends so that if I do become a victim I will feel secure. I will not be so ashamed that I will allow the harassment to continue.

6. I need to be strong. I will develop my own personal style and thereby help reduce the likelihood that

I will be a victim of sexual harassment. I will demonstrate personal power. In fact, I will be a "personal powerhouse." Thus, I will have more choices.

7. If I do become a victim of sexual harassment, I will not allow it to continue. I will not be afraid, nor will I be shamed into silence. The sooner I tell someone in authority, the sooner I do something about it, the less likely I am to be in prolonged personal danger.

8. To defuse situations (because you never know whom you're dealing with), I will not be obnoxious in the case of sexual harassment. I need to remember that it is important to be strong and not take anything that I don't have to, but it might help for me to recall how the Orientals deal with people: If I help someone "save face," I may save my life. In the meantime I can tell my network of family and friends what is going on and maybe have a "bodyguard" for a while. I could take a companion with me wherever I go. I could tell the authorities at my company (or the police) that I am afraid.

9. I need to dress professionally and act in a professional manner on the job. Whether or not this ever has any bearing on a case of sexual harassment, I will feel much better about myself on the job if I look and act professional. At any rate, I will thus never be compromised (in case I am involved in sexual harassment proceedings) by having the testimony reduced to a critique of my clothes.

10. I need to make myself powerful on the job. Bosses have no power unless the people under them are efficient. I need to make myself "indispensable." If they want fast workers, I will be fast. If they

want someone with lots of answers, I will become an "expert." If they want me to be charming, I will develop the power of charisma. Bosses listen to people at the bottom, and I will develop the skills necessary for me to be listened to. I can do that without ever offering any sexual favors. And, if I am fired, I will get another job with or without their recommendation. "There are plenty of fish in the sea."

11. I know that I am good enough to get ahead without giving sex to someone.

12. I am a "personal powerhouse." I understand my own sexuality, and I do not need to prove my sexual ability to anyone. I am very comfortable with my sexuality; in fact, I like myself just like I am.

Dear Diary, I have just written out my own *Devastating Dozen* rules for myself on the job. Can you beat that! Look how far, Dear Diary, I have come in a short time. I think I was really ready to go looking for a personal counselor, Diary, but I don't need one now!

And I can't underestimate how much you've done for me in all this, Diary. You allowed me to express myself openly and as often as I needed to. You have been a mentor to me, a friend and a confidant. How soothing it has been for me to get all of the tangle of wretchedness about this sexual harassment out in the open and down on paper. I would go so far as to say that this is one remedy I would suggest to anyone in a similar mess. It helps to write it all down. It helps you to think clearly and to get your thoughts in order. And—you never yell at me or make me feel like a fool! That has meant a lot. I have never felt embarrassed talking about this to you. Everyone should have such a good friend!

I have learned that I must ask for help when I need it. And I must get the message across to the harasser that I am not going to be involved in sexual harassment, that I know my rights, that I am aware of company policy on the matter of sexual harassment, that I have a whole network of professional people to stand by me, that I have another network of loving family and friends who will support me through anything, that I am not about to be intimidated, and that I will advance in my job according to my own merits. I will let that harasser see what a personal powerhouse I am! In fact, Diary, I have so much to do about my harassment problem that I don't have time to finish this right now ... YOUR PERSONAL POWERHOUSE WILL RETURN

Footnotes

Chapter XI

[1] Sexual Harassment in the Federal Government, Sub-committee on Investigations Hearing, House of Representatives, Washington, DC, 1979, p. 11.

[2] Sexual Harassment, p. 44.

[3] United States Code of Law, Vol. 16, p. 35.

[4] United States Code of Law, pp. 36, 37.

[5] Sexual Harassment in the Federal Government, p. 166.

[6] Bernard Weinraub, New York *Times*, June 20, 1986, pp. 1, 6.

[7] Robert Simison and Cathy Trost, *Wall Street Journal*, June 24, 1986, pp. 1, 27.

[8] Bernard Weinraub

Chapter XII

[1] Simison and Trost.

[2] Simison and Trost.

Bibliography

Fromm, Erich. *Man for Himself: An Inquiry into the Psychology of Ethics.* New York: Fawcett Premier, 1947.

Gilligan, Carol. *In a Different Voice.* Cambridge, Harvard University Press, 1982.

Griffith, Mary. Seminar on "Men and Women Working Together in the Workplace," Louisville, June 20, 1986.

Simison, Robert, and Trost, Cathy. *Wall Street Journal*, June 24, 1986.

Subcommittee Hearing on Sexual Harassment in Federal Government, House of Representatives, 1979.

United States Code of Law, Vol. 16, Washington, DC: U.S. Government Printing Office, 1982.

Weinraub, Bernard. New York *Times*, June 20, 1986.

Index

A

abuse, sexual, 15, 39, 41
acceptance, gaining, 65
action, taking, 14, 24, 25
activity, sexual, 40
advantage, taking, 7
affair, with boss, 5, 21, 54–61
aggression, 38
American Civil Liberties Union, 135
attentions
  enjoying, 3, 16, 60, 65
  homosexual, 21
  unwanted, 131
awareness, sexual, 1, 23

B

behavior
  acceptable, 39
  harassing, 111, 120, 123
  macho, 42
  patterns of, 89–97
Blackmun, Harry A., 118
boss
  attentions of, 1–13
  confrontation with, 3, 6–8
  homosexual, 28–32
  rating, 50
boys, as victims, 78
Brennan, William J., 118

C

Chesnutt, Charles W., 35–36
"circle of light," 79–80
Civil Rights Act of 1964, 114, 118–119,
  123, 132, 139
coach, as harasser, 12, 79
complaint procedure, 22, 112, 113, 132,
  139
conflict, reduction of, 65
confrontation, fear of, 101
Connell, Richard, 67
control
  of one's life, 32

of victim, 36, 43, 48, 137
curruption, of victim, 36
counselor, 17, 18, 47
  school, 10, 18, 24, 56, 77

D

definition, of sexual harassment, 110,
  120, 137–138
discrimination, sex, 114–115, 116–117
double standard, 19
dress
  professional, 129–130, 131, 141
  provocative, 19, 47
drugs, 26, 82

E

egotism, 68
Equal Employment Opportunity
  Commission (EEOC), 135, 136
experience
  lack of, 69
  sexual, 40, 47

F

failure, fear of, 68
Faulkner, William, 41
fear
  of blame, 15
  controlling by, 36
  enjoying another's, 35, 43
  getting involved, 16, 46
  harasser's, 38
  of situation, 4, 5, 9
feedback, of advice, 9, 10, 12, 49
feelings, rating one's, 49–50
flattery, by attention, 1, 9
Freud, Sigmund, 69, 127
Fromm, Erich, 99, 105

G

Gilman, Charlotte, Perkins, 66
greed, 68

guilelessness, 68
gullibility, 68

H

harasser, views of, 34–44, 48
hatred, of victim, 36, 48
homosexuals, 128
   harassment by, 127
   harassment of, 128, 138
   resources for, 135
Housing and Urban Development,
   Department of, 109
Human Rights, Commission on, 135

I

inadequacy, feeling of, 68
inducement, 111, 122, 125, 137
International Union of Electrical and
   Machine Workers (IUE), 110
investigation, Congressional, 109–111

J

"jailbait," 40
jealousy, 15, 29, 46, 75
job
   firing from, 2, 60, 112, 113
   first, 1, 9, 40
   getting new, 12
   needing, 17, 127
   part-time, 54–61
   private, 28–30
   quitting, 2, 5, 14, 85
   security, 65
Jung, Carl, 69, 80

L

Lenhoff, Donna, 109–110
lesbian, 60
   harassment by, 127
   resources for, 135
lust, 39, 41, 42–43, 48, 80, 128, 137
lying, accusation of, 3, 56

M

marriage, promise of, 5, 75–76
Marshall, Thurgood, 118
maturity, feeling of, 4, 10

Maupassant, Guy de, 66
media, 38, 39, 41, 42
meditation, 80
men, as victims, 64, 81–82, 138
Merit Systems Protection Board, 116
Miller vs. *Bank of America*, 117
molestation, child, 41
murder, 25, 30–31, 43, 45, 48, 111, 136,
   137

N

networking, 134, 140

O

object, sexual, 39, 42, 44

P

parents
   hurting, 28, 30, 58
   rating, 51
   suspicions of, 76
   telling, 1, 2, 9, 15, 17, 30, 47
passivity, 101
perpetrator, 41–44
police, as harassers, 87
pronography, child, 41, 78
possessiveness, 68
power
   connotations of, 103, 105
   exerting, 35, 39, 48, 64, 128, 137
   personal, 99, 100–108, 109, 133–134,
      141
   sexual, 37, 43
predator, harasser as, 35, 37, 38–39
problem
   dealing with, 12
   perspective on, 18, 47
productivity, personal, 105, 107
promotion, as reward, 65

R

rape, 18, 25, 43, 45, 48, 86, 111, 136, 137
recommendation, 9, 14, 65, 112
Rehnquist, William H., 117–118, 119
relationship
   lesbian, 61
   master/slave, 37

remarks, embarrassing, 10, 17
reporting, to superiors, 7, 24
résumé, building a good, 2, 9, 112
rewards
    in harassment, 2, 8, 36, 65, 123
    of job, 51
rite of passage, 41

S

scenarios, for confronting boss, 6–8
school
    cutting, 28, 30
    failing, 29, 56–57
    harassment in, 73, 83, 123–124
    as workplace, 124
self-confidence, lack of, 68
self-image, poor, 68
self-protection, 79
self-respect, 5
self-survey, 89–97
skills
    inventory, 89–97
    personality, 97–98
slave trade, child, 41
Somson, Barbara, 110
sophistication, teenage, 1, 3, 10, 19–20,
    81
status, gaining, 65
Stevens, John Paul, 118
stress, 7, 112, 128, 133
style, power as, 103–104, 109
suicide, 5, 62, 67
suit, bringing, 8, 83, 84, 125
superego, 70
Supreme Court, U.S., 117–118

system, victim of, 38

T

teacher
    as harasser, 73, 78, 84
    as victim, 88
touching, unwanted, 2, 7, 10, 11, 14, 24,
    83, 110–111
training, employer-sponsored, 113, 139
trust
    losing, 3, 11
    misplaced, 67

V

victim, 12, 35, 37, 39
    harasser as, 38–39, 41, 80
    view of, 63–72
Vinson vs. Meritor, 117, 119, 122, 131
violence, 36, 43, 48, 111, 128, 137
virginity, 40

W

Watts, Alan, 70
women
    as harassers, 84. 127
    home as workplace of, 124
    resources of, 134
    as second-class citizens, 63–64
    as victims, 138
Women's Legal Defense Fund, 109–110

Y

young, as sex partners, 39–40, 41